U. S. Fish & Wildlife Service

Adaptive Harvest Management

2004 Hunting Season

PREFACE

The process of setting waterfowl hunting regulations is conducted annually in the United States (Blohm 1989). This process involves a number of meetings where the status of waterfowl is reviewed by the agencies responsible for setting hunting regulations. In addition, the U.S. Fish and Wildlife Service (USFWS) publishes proposed regulations in the *Federal Register* to allow public comment. This document is part of a series of reports intended to support development of harvest regulations for the 2004 hunting season. Specifically, this report is intended to provide waterfowl managers and the public with information about the use of adaptive harvest management (AHM) for setting duck-hunting regulations in the United States. This report provides the most current data, analyses, and decision-making protocols. However, adaptive management is a dynamic process and some information presented in this report will differ from that in previous reports.

Citation:	U.S. Fish and Wildlife Service. 2004. Adaptive Harvest Management: 2004 Hunting Season. U.S. Dept. Interior, Washington, D.C. 39pp.

ACKNOWLEDGMENTS

A working group comprised of representatives from the USFWS, the Canadian Wildlife Service (CWS), and the four Flyway Councils (Appendix A) was established in 1992 to review the scientific basis for managing waterfowl harvests. The working group, supported by technical experts from the waterfowl management and research community, subsequently proposed a framework for adaptive harvest management, which was first implemented in 1995. The USFWS expresses its gratitude to the AHM Working Group and to the many other individuals, organizations, and agencies that have contributed to the development and implementation of AHM.

This report was prepared by the USFWS Division of Migratory Bird Management. F. A. Johnson, G. S. Boomer, and J. A. Royle were the principal authors. Individuals that provided essential information or otherwise assisted with report preparation were D. J. Case (D.J. Case & Assoc.), M. J. Conroy (U.S. Geological Survey [USGS]), R. V. Raftovich (USFWS), M. C. Runge (USGS), and K. A. Wilkins (USFWS). Comments regarding this document should be sent to the Chief, Division of Migratory Bird Management - USFWS, 4401 North Fairfax Drive, MS MSP-4107, Arlington, VA 22203.

Cover art:	A portion of Scot Storm's painting of redheads (*Aythya americana*), which was chosen for the 2004 federal "duck stamp."

TABLE OF CONTENTS

EXECUTIVE SUMMARY

In 1995 the U.S. Fish and Wildlife Service (USFWS) implemented the Adaptive Harvest Management (AHM) program for setting duck hunting regulations in the United States. The AHM approach provides a framework for making objective decisions in the face of incomplete knowledge concerning waterfowl population dynamics and regulatory impacts.

The original AHM protocol was based solely on the dynamics of midcontinent mallards, but efforts are being made to account for mallards breeding eastward and westward of the midcontinent region. The challenge for managers is to vary hunting regulations among Flyways in a manner that recognizes each Flyway's unique breeding-ground derivation of mallards. For the 2004 hunting season, the USFWS will continue to consider a regulatory choice for the Atlantic Flyway that depends exclusively on the status of eastern mallards. This arrangement continues to be considered provisional, however, until the implications of this approach are better understood. The prescribed regulatory choice for the Mississippi, Central, and Pacific Flyways continues to depend exclusively on the status of midcontinent mallards. Investigations of the dynamics of western mallards (and their potential effect on regulations in the West) are continuing and the USFWS is not yet prepared to recommend an AHM protocol for this mallard stock.

The mallard population models that are the basis for prescribing hunting regulations were revised extensively in 2002. These revised models account for an apparent positive bias in estimates of survival and reproductive rates, and also allow for alternative hypotheses concerning the effects of harvest and the environment in regulating population size. Model-specific weights reflect the relative confidence in alternative hypotheses, and are updated annually using comparisons of predicted and observed population sizes. For midcontinent mallards, current model weights favor the weakly density-dependent reproductive hypothesis (91%). Evidence for the additive-mortality hypothesis remains equivocal (58%). For eastern mallards, current model weights favor the strongly density-dependent reproductive hypothesis (72%). By consensus, hunting mortality is assumed to be additive in eastern mallards.

For the 2004 hunting season, the USFWS is continuing to consider the same regulatory alternatives as last year. The nature of the restrictive, moderate, and liberal alternatives has remained essentially unchanged since 1997, except that extended framework dates have been offered in the moderate and liberal alternatives since 2002. Also, at the request of the Flyway Councils the USFWS has agreed to exclude closed duck-hunting seasons from the AHM protocol when the breeding-population size of midcontinent mallards is ≥5.5 million (traditional survey area plus the Great Lakes region).

Harvest rates associated with the each of the regulatory alternatives are predicted using Bayesian statistical methods. Essentially, the idea is to use historical information to develop initial harvest-rate predictions, to make regulatory decisions based on those predictions, and then to observe realized harvest rates. Those observed harvest rates, in turn, are used to update the predictions. Using this approach, predictions of harvest rates of midcontinent mallards under the regulatory alternatives have been updated based on band-reporting rate studies conducted since 1998. Results from the 2002 and 2003 hunting seasons suggest that extended framework dates result in a mean marginal increase in harvest rates of adult-male midcontinent mallards of 0.0129, which is similar to what was expected. It is not feasible to update estimates of eastern-mallard harvest rates until additional band-reporting rate studies are conducted and analyzed.

Optimal regulatory strategies for the 2004 hunting season were calculated using: (1) harvest-management objectives specific to each mallard stock; (2) the 2004 regulatory alternatives; and (3) current population models and associated weights for midcontinent and eastern mallards. Based on this year's survey results of 8.36 million midcontinent mallards (traditional survey area plus MN, WI, and MI), 2.51 million ponds in Prairie Canada, and 1.11 million eastern mallards, the optimal regulatory choice for all four Flyways is the liberal alternative.

The USFWS is continuing discussions with the AHM Working Group, Flyway Councils, States, and others about future development and application of AHM. The International Association of Fish and Wildlife Agencies has convened an AHM task force, comprised of recognized leaders in waterfowl management, to help provide policy guidance regarding the nature of harvest-management objectives and regulatory alternatives. Moreover, progress is gradually being made to extend the decision-making framework of AHM to other species, including black ducks, scaup, pintails, and the Atlantic Population of Canada geese.

BACKGROUND

The annual process of setting duck-hunting regulations in the United States is based on a system of resource monitoring, data analyses, and rule-making (Blohm 1989). Each year, monitoring activities such as aerial surveys and hunter questionnaires provide information on population size, habitat conditions, and harvest levels. Data collected from this monitoring program are analyzed each year, and proposals for duck-hunting regulations are developed by the Flyway Councils, States, and USFWS. After extensive public review, the USFWS announces regulatory guidelines within which States can set their hunting seasons.

In 1995, the USFWS adopted the concept of adaptive resource management (Walters 1986) for regulating duck harvests in the United States. This approach explicitly recognizes that the consequences of hunting regulations cannot be predicted with certainty, and provides a framework for making objective decisions in the face of that uncertainty (Williams and Johnson 1995). Inherent in the adaptive approach is an awareness that management performance can be maximized only if regulatory effects can be predicted reliably. Thus, adaptive management relies on an iterative cycle of monitoring, assessment, and decision-making to clarify the relationships among hunting regulations, harvests, and waterfowl abundance.

In regulating waterfowl harvests, managers face four fundamental sources of uncertainty (Nichols et al. 1995, Johnson et al. 1996, Williams et al. 1996):

(1)   environmental variation - the temporal and spatial variation in weather conditions and other key features of waterfowl habitat; an example is the annual change in the number of ponds in the Prairie Pothole Region, where water conditions influence duck reproductive success;

(2)   partial controllability - the ability of managers to control harvest only within limits; the harvest resulting from a particular set of hunting regulations cannot be predicted with certainty because of variation in weather conditions, timing of migration, hunter effort, and other factors;

(3)   partial observability - the ability to estimate key population attributes (e.g., population size, reproductive rate, harvest) only within the precision afforded by extant monitoring programs; and

(4)   structural uncertainty - an incomplete understanding of biological processes; a familiar example is the long-standing debate about whether harvest is additive to other sources of mortality or whether populations compensate for hunting losses through reduced natural mortality. Structural uncertainty increases contentiousness in the decision-making process and decreases the extent to which managers can meet long-term conservation goals.

AHM was developed as a systematic process for dealing objectively with these uncertainties. The key components of AHM include (Johnson et al. 1993, Williams and Johnson 1995):

(1)   a limited number of regulatory alternatives, which describe Flyway-specific season lengths, bag limits, and framework dates;

(2)   a set of population models describing various hypotheses about the effects of harvest and environmental factors on waterfowl abundance;

(3)   a measure of reliability (probability or "weight") for each population model; and

(4)   a mathematical description of the objective(s) of harvest management (i.e., an "objective function"), by which alternative regulatory strategies can be compared.

These components are used in a stochastic optimization procedure to derive a regulatory strategy. A regulatory strategy specifies the optimal regulatory choice, with respect to the stated management objectives, for each possible combination of breeding population size, environmental conditions, and model weights (Johnson et al. 1997). The setting of annual hunting regulations then involves an iterative process:

(1)   each year, an optimal regulatory choice is identified based on resource and environmental conditions, and on current model weights;

(2)   after the regulatory decision is made, model-specific predictions for subsequent breeding population size are determined;

(3)   when monitoring data become available, model weights are increased to the extent that observations of population size agree with predictions, and decreased to the extent that they disagree; and

4

(4)   the new model weights are used to start another iteration of the process.

By iteratively updating model weights and optimizing regulatory choices, the process should eventually identify which model is the best overall predictor of changes in population abundance. The process is optimal in the sense that it provides the regulatory choice each year necessary to maximize management performance. It is adaptive in the sense that the harvest strategy "evolves" to account for new knowledge generated by a comparison of predicted and observed population sizes.

MALLARD STOCKS AND FLYWAY MANAGEMENT

Since its inception, AHM has focused on the population dynamics and harvest potential of mallards, especially those breeding in midcontinent North America. Mallards constitute a large portion of the total U.S. duck harvest, and traditionally have been a reliable indicator of the status of many other species. As management capabilities have grown, there has been increasing interest in the ecology and management of breeding mallards that occur outside the midcontinent region. Geographic differences in the reproduction, mortality, and migrations of mallard stocks suggest that there may be corresponding differences in optimal levels of sport harvest. The ability to regulate harvests of mallards originating from various breeding areas is complicated, however, by the fact that a large degree of mixing occurs during the hunting season. The challenge for managers, then, is to vary hunting regulations among Flyways in a manner that recognizes each Flyway's unique breeding-ground derivation of mallards. Of course, no Flyway receives mallards exclusively from one breeding area, and so Flyway-specific harvest strategies ideally must account for multiple breeding stocks that are exposed to a common harvest.

The optimization procedures used in AHM can account for breeding populations of mallards beyond the midcontinent region, and for the manner in which these ducks distribute themselves among the Flyways during the hunting season. An optimal approach would allow for Flyway-specific regulatory strategies, which in a sense represent for each Flyway an average of the optimal harvest strategies for each contributing breeding stock, weighted by the relative size of each stock in the fall flight. This "joint optimization" of multiple mallard stocks requires:

(1)   models of population dynamics for all recognized stocks of mallards;
(2)   an objective function that accounts for harvest-management goals for all mallard stocks in the aggregate; and
(3)   decision rules allowing Flyway-specific regulatory choices.

Joint optimization of multiple stocks presents many challenges in terms of population modeling, parameter estimation, and computation of regulatory strategies. These challenges cannot always be overcome due to limitations in monitoring and assessment programs, and in access to sufficient computing resources. In some cases, it may be possible to impose constraints or assumptions that simplify the problem. Although sub-optimal by design, these constrained regulatory strategies may perform nearly as well as those that are optimal, particularly in cases where breeding stocks differ little in their ability to support harvest, where Flyways do not receive significant numbers of birds from more than one breeding stock, or where management outcomes are highly uncertain.

Currently, two stocks of mallards are officially recognized for the purposes of AHM (Fig. 1). We continue to use a constrained approach to the optimization of these stocks' harvest, whereby the Atlantic Flyway regulatory strategy is based exclusively on the status of eastern mallards, and the regulatory strategy for the remaining Flyways is based exclusively on the status of midcontinent mallards. This approach has been determined to perform nearly as well as a joint-optimization approach because mixing of the two stocks during the hunting season is limited. However, the approach continues to be considered provisional until its implications are better understood.

MALLARD POPULATION DYNAMICS

Midcontinent Mallards

Population size.--For the purposes of AHM, midcontinent mallards are defined as those breeding in federal survey strata 1-18, 20-50, and 75-77 (i.e., the "traditional" survey area), and in Minnesota, Wisconsin, and Michigan. Estimates of the abundance of this midcontinent population are available only since 1992 (Table 1).

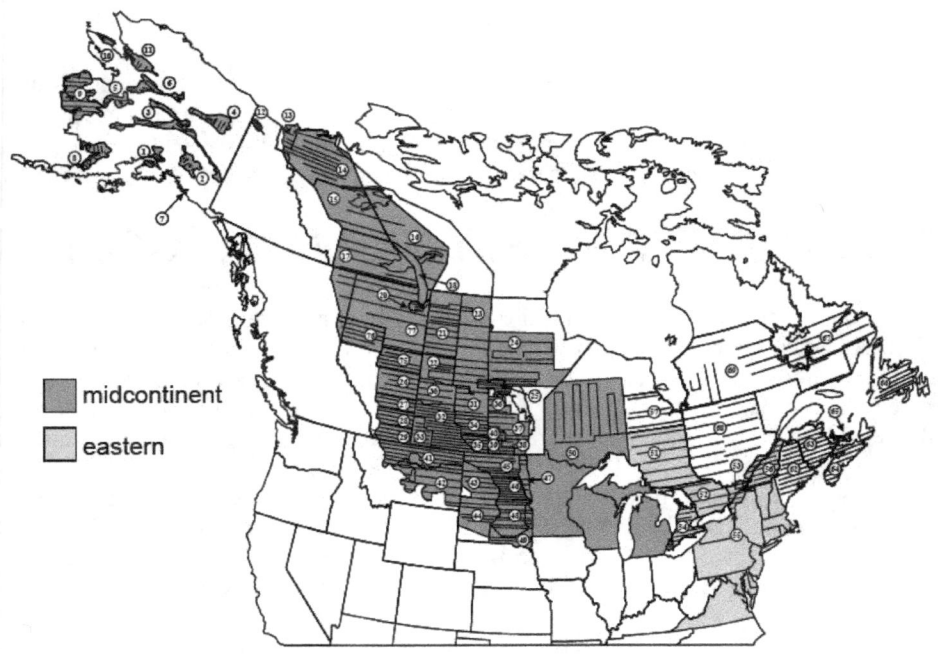

Fig. 1. Survey areas currently assigned to the midcontinent and eastern stocks of mallards for the purposes of AHM. Delineation of the western-mallard stock is pending a review of population monitoring programs.

Table 1. Estimates (N) and standard errors (SE) of mallards (in millions) in spring in the traditional survey area (strata 1-18, 20-50, and 75-77) and the states of Minnesota, Wisconsin, and Michigan.

Year	Traditional surveys		State surveys		Total	
	N	SE	N	SE	N	SE
1992	5.9761	0.2410	0.9946	0.1597	6.9706	0.2891
1993	5.7083	0.2089	0.9347	0.1457	6.6430	0.2547
1994	6.9801	0.2828	1.1505	0.1163	8.1306	0.3058
1995	8.2694	0.2875	1.1214	0.1965	9.3908	0.3482
1996	7.9413	0.2629	1.0251	0.1443	8.9664	0.2999
1997	9.9397	0.3085	1.0777	0.1445	11.0174	0.3407
1998	9.6404	0.3016	1.1224	0.1792	10.7628	0.3508
1999	10.8057	0.3445	1.0591	0.2122	11.8648	0.4046
2000	9.4702	0.2902	1.2350	0.1761	10.7052	0.3395
2001	7.9040	0.2269	0.8622	0.1086	8.7662	0.2516
2002	7.5037	0.2465	1.0820	0.1152	8.5857	0.2721
2003	7.9497	0.2673	0.8360	0.0734	8.7857	0.2772
2004	7.4253	0.2820	0.9333	0.0748	8.3586	0.2917

Population models.-In 2002 we extensively revised the set of alternative models describing the population dynamics of midcontinent mallards (Runge et al. 2002, USFWS 2002). Collectively, the models express uncertainty (or disagreement) about whether harvest is an additive or compensatory form of mortality (Burnham et al. 1984), and whether the reproductive process is weakly or strongly density-dependent (i.e., the degree to which reproductive rates decline with increasing population size).

All population models for midcontinent mallards share a common "balance equation" to predict changes in breeding-population size as a function of annual survival and reproductive rates:

$$N_{t+1} = N_t \left(m S_{t,AM} + (1-m) \left(S_{t,AF} + R_t \left(S_{t,JF} + S_{t,JM} \, \phi_F^{sum} / \phi_M^{sum} \right) \right) \right)$$

where:
N = breeding population size,
m = proportion of males in the breeding population,
S_{AM}, S_{AF}, S_{JF}, and S_{JM} = survival rates of adult males, adult females, young females, and young males, respectively,
R = reproductive rate, defined as the fall age ratio of females,
$\phi_F^{sum} / \phi_M^{sum}$ = the ratio of female (F) to male (M) summer survival, and
t = year.

We assumed that m and $\phi_F^{sum} / \phi_M^{sum}$ are fixed and known. We also assumed, based in part on information provided by Blohm et al. (1987), that the ratio of female to male summer survival was equivalent to the ratio of annual survival rates in the absence of harvest. Based on this assumption, we estimated $\phi_F^{sum} / \phi_M^{sum} = 0.897$. To estimate m we expressed the balance equation in matrix form:

$$\begin{bmatrix} N_{t+1,AM} \\ N_{t+1,AF} \end{bmatrix} = \begin{bmatrix} S_{AM} & RS_{JM} \, \phi_F^{sum} / \phi_M^{sum} \\ 0 & S_{AF} + RS_{JF} \end{bmatrix} \begin{bmatrix} N_{t,AM} \\ N_{t,AF} \end{bmatrix}$$

and substituted the constant ratio of summer survival and mean values of estimated annual survival and reproductive rates. The right eigenvector of the transition matrix is the stable sex structure that the breeding population eventually would attain with these constant demographic rates. This eigenvector yielded an estimate of $m = 0.5246$.

Using estimates of annual survival and reproductive rates, the balance equation for midcontinent mallards over-predicted observed population sizes by 10.8% on average. The source of the bias is unknown, so we modified the balance equation to eliminate the bias by adjusting both survival and reproductive rates:

$$N_{t+1} = \gamma_S N_t \left(m S_{t,AM} + (1-m) \left(S_{t,AF} + \gamma_R R_t \left(S_{t,JF} + S_{t,JM} \, \phi_F^{sum} / \phi_M^{sum} \right) \right) \right)$$

where γ denotes the bias-correction factors for survival (S) and reproduction (R). We used a least squares approach to estimate $\gamma_S = 0.9479$ and $\gamma_R = 0.8620$.

Survival process.-We considered two alternative hypotheses for the relationship between annual survival and harvest rates. For both models, we assumed that survival in the absence of harvest was the same for adults and young of the same sex. In the model where harvest mortality is additive to natural mortality:

$$S_{t,sex,age} = s_{0,sex}^A \left(1 - K_{t,sex,age} \right)$$

and in the model where changes in natural mortality compensate for harvest losses (up to some threshold):

$$S_{t,sex,age} = \begin{cases} s_{0,sex}^{C} & if \ K_{t,sex,age} \leq 1 - s_{0,sex}^{C} \\ 1 - K_{t,sex,age} & if \ K_{t,sex,age} > 1 - s_{0,sex}^{C} \end{cases}$$

where s_0 = survival in the absence of harvest under the additive (A) or compensatory (C) model, and K = harvest rate adjusted for crippling loss (20%, Anderson and Burnham 1976). We averaged estimates of s_0 across banding reference areas by weighting by breeding-population size. For the additive model, s_0 = 0.7896 and 0.6886 for males and females, respectively. For the compensatory model, s_0 = 0.6467 and 0.5965 for males and females, respectively. These estimates may seem counterintuitive because survival in the absence of harvest should be the same for both models. However, estimating a common (but still sex-specific) s_0 for both models leads to alternative models that do not fit available band-recovery data equally well. More importantly, it suggests that the greatest uncertainty about survival rates is when harvest rate is within the realm of experience. By allowing s_0 to differ between additive and compensatory models, we more acknowledge that the greatest uncertainty about survival rate is its value in the absence of harvest (i.e., where we have no experience).

Reproductive process.–Annual reproductive rates were estimated from age ratios in the harvest of females, corrected using a constant estimate of differential vulnerability. Predictor variables were the number of ponds in May in Prairie Canada (P, in millions) and the size of the breeding population (N, in millions). We estimated the best-fitting linear model, and then calculated the 80% confidence ellipsoid for all model parameters. We chose the two points on this ellipsoid with the largest and smallest values for the effect of breeding-population size, and generated a weakly density-dependent model:

$$R_t = 0.7166 + 0.1083P_t - 0.0373N_t$$

and a strongly density-dependent model:

$$R_t = 1.1390 + 0.1376P_t - 0.1131N_t$$

Pond dynamics.–We modeled annual variation in Canadian pond numbers as a first-order autoregressive process. The estimated model was:

$$P_{t+1} = 2.2127 + 0.3420P_t + \varepsilon_t$$

where ponds are in millions and ε_t is normally distributed with mean = 0 and variance = 1.2567.

Variance of prediction errors.–Using the balance equation and submodels described above, predictions of breeding-population size in year $t+1$ depend only on specification of population size, pond numbers, and harvest rate in year t. For the period in which comparisons were possible, we compared these predictions with observed population sizes.

We estimated the prediction-error variance by setting:

$$e_t = \ln\left(N_t^{obs}\right) - \ln\left(N_t^{pre}\right)$$

then assuming $\quad e_t \sim N\left(0, \sigma^2\right)$

and estimating $\quad \hat{\sigma}^2 = \sum_t \left[\ln\left(N_t^{obs}\right) - \ln\left(N_t^{pre}\right)\right]^2 \Big/ (n-1)$

where *obs* and *pre* are observed and predicted population sizes (in millions), respectively, and n = the number of years being compared. We were concerned about a variance estimate that was too small, either by chance or because the number of years in which comparisons were possible was small. Therefore, we calculated the upper 80% confidence limit for σ^2 based on a Chi-squared distribution for each combination of the alternative survival and reproductive sub-models, and then averaged them. The final estimate of σ^2 was 0.0243, equivalent to a coefficient of variation of about 17%.

Model implications.–The set of alternative population models suggests that carrying capacity (average population size in the absence of harvest) for an average number of Canadian ponds is somewhere between about 6 and 16 million mallards. The population model with additive hunting mortality and weakly density-dependent recruitment (SaRw) leads to the most conservative harvest strategy, whereas the model with compensatory hunting mortality and strongly density-dependent recruitment (ScRs) leads to the most liberal strategy. The other two models (SaRs and ScRw) lead to strategies that are intermediate between these extremes. Under the models with compensatory hunting mortality (ScRs and ScRw), the optimal strategy is to have a liberal regulation regardless of population size or number of ponds because at harvest rates achieved under the liberal alternative, harvest has no effect on population size. Under the strongly density-dependent model (ScRs), the density-dependence regulates the population and keeps it within narrow bounds. Under the weakly density-dependent model (ScRw), the density-dependence does not exert as strong a regulatory effect, and the population size fluctuates more.

Model weights.--Model weights are calculated as Bayesian probabilities, reflecting the relative ability of the individual alternative models to predict observed changes in population size. The Bayesian probability for each model is a function of the model's previous (or prior) weight and the likelihood of the observed population size under that model. We used Bayes' theorem to calculate model weights from a comparison of predicted and observed population sizes for the years 1996-2004, starting with equal model weights in 1995. For the purposes of updating, we predicted breeding-population size in the traditional survey area in year $t + 1$, from breeding-population size, Canadian ponds, and harvest rates in year t.

Model weights changed little until all models under-predicted the change in population size from 1998 to 1999, perhaps indicating there is a significant factor affecting population dynamics that is absent from all four models (Table 2). Throughout the period of updating model weights, there has been no clear preference for either the additive (58%) or compensatory (42%) mortality models. For the last several years, model weights favor the weakly density-dependent (91%) reproductive model over the strongly density-dependent (9%) one. The reader is warned, however, that models can sometimes make reliable predictions of population size for reasons having little to do with the biological hypotheses expressed therein (Johnson et al. 2002*b*).

Inclusion of mallards in the Great Lakes region.--Model development originally did not include mallards breeding in the states of Wisconsin, Minnesota, and Michigan, primarily because full data sets were not available from these areas to allow appropriate analysis. However, mallards in the Great Lakes region have been included in the midcontinent mallard AHM protocol since 1997 by assuming that population dynamics for these mallards are similar to those in the traditional survey area. Based on that assumption, predictions of breeding population size are scaled up to reflect inclusion of mallards in the Great Lakes region. From 1992 through 2004, when population estimates were available for all three states, the average proportion of the total midcontinent mallard population that was in the Great Lakes region was 0.1151 (SD = 0.0183). We assumed a normal distribution with these parameter values to make the conversion between the traditional survey area and total breeding-population size.

Table 2. Model-specific predictions and weights for midcontinent mallards (ScRs = compensatory mortality and strongly density-dependent reproduction, ScRw = compensatory mortality and weakly density-dependent reproduction, SaRs = additive mortality and strongly density-dependent reproduction, and SaRw = additive mortality and weakly density-dependent reproduction). Model weights were assumed to be equal in 1995.

Year	Bpop(t)[a]	Ponds(t)[b]	Harvest rate(t)[c]		Model ScRs	ScRw	SaRs	SaRw	Observed bpop(t+1)[a]
1995	8.2694	3.8925	0.1198	predicted bpop(t+1):	7.6740	8.0153	7.7037	8.0280	7.9413
				weight(t+1):	0.2469	0.2525	0.2482	0.2524	
1996	7.9413	5.0026	0.1184	predicted bpop(t+1):	8.0580	8.1776	8.0702	8.1841	9.9397
				weight(t+1):	0.2305	0.2666	0.2348	0.2681	
1997	9.9397	5.0610	0.1171	predicted bpop(t+1):	9.0964	9.9258	9.1763	9.9689	9.6404
				weight(t+1):	0.2235	0.2722	0.2320	0.2723	
1998	9.6404	2.5217	0.1102	predicted bpop(t+1):	7.4334	8.4655	7.6474	8.6478	10.8057
				weight(t+1):	0.0596	0.3799	0.0942	0.4664	
1999	10.8057	3.8620	0.1002	predicted bpop(t+1):	8.5916	9.9905	8.9505	10.3341	9.4702
				weight(t+1):	0.0548	0.4006	0.0987	0.4459	
2000	9.4702	2.4222	0.1264	predicted bpop(t+1):	7.3262	8.2969	7.3621	8.2718	7.9040
				weight(t+1):	0.0514	0.4032	0.0940	0.4514	
2001	7.9040	2.7472	0.1075	predicted bpop(t+1):	6.9153	7.2626	7.0940	7.4325	7.5040
				weight(t+1):	0.0458	0.4034	0.0901	0.4607	
2002	7.5040	1.4390	0.1133	predicted bpop(t+1):	6.1036	6.4607	6.2323	6.5763	7.9497
				weight(t+1):	0.0257	0.3928	0.0628	0.5187	
2003	7.9497	3.522	0.1134	predicted bpop(t+1):	7.3237	7.6031	7.4273	7.6964	7.4253
				weight(t+1):	0.0261	0.3955	0.0639	0.5145	

[a] Breeding population size (in millions) in the traditional survey area only (i.e., does not include Minnesota, Michigan, and Wisconsin) in year t.
[b] Ponds (in millions) in May in Prairie Canada.
[c] Harvest rate of adult-male midcontinent mallards. Rates for 1995 and 1998-2003 are empirical estimates. Rates for 1996 and 1997 are predictions based on models describing the historical relationship between regulations and harvest rate.

Eastern Mallards

Population size.--For purposes of AHM, eastern mallards are defined as those breeding in southern Ontario and Quebec (federal survey strata 51-54 and 56) and in the northeastern U.S. (state plot surveys; Heusmann and Sauer 2000) (see Fig. 1).

Estimates of population size have varied from 856 thousand to 1.1 million since 1990, with the majority of the population accounted for in the northeastern U.S. (Table 3).

Table 3. Estimates (N) and associated standard errors (SE) of mallards (in thousands) in spring in the northeastern U.S. (state plot surveys) and eastern Canada (federal survey strata 51-54 and 56).

Year	State surveys		Federal surveys		Total	
	N	SE	N	SE	N	SE
1990	665.1	78.3	190.7	47.2	855.8	91.4
1991	779.2	88.3	152.8	33.7	932.0	94.5
1992	562.2	47.9	320.3	53.0	882.5	71.5
1993	683.1	49.7	292.1	48.2	975.2	69.3
1994	853.1	62.7	219.5	28.2	1072.5	68.7
1995	862.8	70.2	184.4	40.0	1047.2	80.9
1996	848.4	61.1	283.1	55.7	1131.5	82.6
1997	795.1	49.6	212.1	39.6	1007.2	63.4
1998	775.1	49.7	263.8	67.2	1038.9	83.6
1999	879.7	60.2	212.5	36.9	1092.2	70.6
2000	757.8	48.5	132.3	26.4	890.0	55.2
2001	807.5	51.4	200.2	35.6	1007.7	62.5
2002	834.1	56.2	171.3	30.0	1005.4	63.8
2003	731.8	47.0	308.3	55.4	1040.1	72.6
2004	809.1	51.8	301.5	53.3	1110.7	74.3

Population models.–We also revised the population models for eastern mallards in 2002 (Johnson et al. 2002*a*, USFWS 2002). The current set of six models: (1) relies solely on federal and state waterfowl surveys (rather than the Breeding Bird Survey) to predict reproductive rates; (2) allows for the possibility of a positive bias in estimates of survival or reproductive rates; (3) incorporates competing hypotheses of strongly and weakly density-dependent reproduction; and (4) assumes that hunting mortality is additive to other sources of mortality.

As with midcontinent mallards, all population models for eastern mallards share a common balance equation to predict changes in breeding-population size as a function of annual survival and reproductive rates:

$$N_{t+1} = N_t \cdot \left(\left(p \cdot S_t^{am} \right) + \left((1-p) \cdot S_t^{af} \right) + \left(p \cdot \left(A_t^m / d \right) \cdot S_t^{ym} \right) + \left(p \cdot \left(A_t^m / d \right) \cdot \psi \cdot S_t^{yf} \right) \right)$$

where:
N = breeding-population size,
p = proportion of males in the breeding population,
S^{am}, S^{af}, S^{ym}, and S^{yf} = survival rates of adult males, adult females, young males, and young females, respectively,
A^m = ratio of young males to adult males in the harvest,
d = ratio of young male to adult male direct recovery rates,
ψ = the ratio of male to female summer survival, and
t = year.

In this balance equation, we assume that p, d, and ψ are fixed and known. The parameter ψ is necessary to account for the difference in anniversary date between the breeding-population survey (May) and the survival and reproductive rate estimates (August). This model also assumes that the sex ratio of fledged young is 1:1; hence A^m/d appears twice in the balance equation. We estimated $d = 1.043$ as the median ratio of young:adult male band-recovery rates in those states from which wing receipts were obtained. We estimated $\psi = 1.216$ by regressing through the origin estimates of male survival against female survival in the absence of harvest, assuming that differences in natural mortality between males and females occur principally in summer. To estimate p, we used a population projection matrix of the form:

$$\begin{bmatrix} M_{t+1} \\ F_{t+1} \end{bmatrix} = \begin{bmatrix} S^{am} + \left(A^m/d \right) \cdot S^{ym} & 0 \\ \left(A^m/d \right) \cdot \psi \cdot S^{yf} & S^{af} \end{bmatrix} \begin{bmatrix} M_{t+1} \\ F_{t+1} \end{bmatrix}$$

where M and F are the relative number of males and females in the breeding populations, respectively. To parameterize the projection matrix we used average annual survival rate and age ratio estimates, and the estimates of d and ψ provided above. The right eigenvector of the projection matrix is the stable proportion of males and females the breeding population eventually would attain in the face of constant demographic rates. This eigenvector yielded an estimate of $p = 0.544$.

We also attempted to determine whether estimates of survival and reproductive rates were unbiased. We relied on the balance equation provided above, except that we included additional parameters to correct for any bias that might exist. Because we were unsure of the source(s) of potential bias, we alternatively assumed that any bias resided solely in survival rates:

$$N_{t+1} = N_t \cdot \Omega \cdot \left(\left(p \cdot S_t^{am} \right) + \left((1-p) \cdot S_t^{af} \right) + \left(p \cdot \left(A_t^m/d \right) \cdot S_t^{ym} \right) + \left(p \cdot \left(A_t^m/d \right) \cdot \psi \cdot S_t^{yf} \right) \right)$$

(where Ω is the bias-correction factor for survival rates), or solely in reproductive rates:

$$N_{t+1} = N_t \cdot \left(\left(p \cdot S_t^{am} \right) + \left((1-p) \cdot S_t^{af} \right) + \left(p \cdot \alpha \cdot \left(A_t^m/d \right) \cdot S_t^{ym} \right) + \left(p \cdot \alpha \cdot \left(A_t^m/d \right) \cdot \psi \cdot S_t^{yf} \right) \right)$$

(where α is the bias-correction factor for reproductive rates). We estimated Ω and α by determining the values of these parameters that minimized the sum of squared differences between observed and predicted population sizes. Based on this analysis, $\Omega = 0.836$ and $\alpha = 0.701$, suggesting a positive bias in survival or reproductive rates. However, because of the limited number of years available for comparing observed and predicted population sizes, we also retained the balance equation that assumes estimates of survival and reproductive rates are unbiased.

Survival process.–For purposes of AHM, annual survival rates must be predicted based on the specification of regulation-specific harvest rates (and perhaps on other uncontrolled factors). Annual survival for each age (i) and sex (j) class under a given regulatory alternative is:

$$S_t^{i,j} = \overline{\theta}^{\,j} \cdot \left(1 - \frac{\left(h_t^{am} \cdot v^{i,j} \right)}{(1-c)} \right)$$

where:
S = annual survival,
$\overline{\theta}^{\,j}$ = mean survival from natural causes,
h^{am} = harvest rate of adult males, and
v = harvest vulnerability relative to adult males,
c = rate of crippling (unretrieved harvest).

This model assumes that annual variation in survival is due solely to variation in harvest rates, that relative harvest vulnerability of the different age-sex classes is fixed and known, and that survival from natural causes is fixed at its sample mean. We estimated $\overline{\theta}^{\,j} = 0.7307$ and 0.5950 for males and females, respectively.

Reproductive process.–As with survival, annual reproductive rates must be predicted in advance of setting regulations. We relied on the apparent relationship between breeding-population size and reproductive rates:

$$R_t = a \cdot \exp\left(b \cdot N_t\right)$$

where R_t is the reproductive rate (i.e., A_t^m / d), N_t is breeding-population size in millions, and a and b are model parameters. The least-squares parameter estimates were $a = 2.508$ and $b = -0.875$. Because of both the importance and uncertainty of the relationship between population size and reproduction, we specified two alternative models in which the slope (b) was fixed at the least-squares estimate ± one standard error, and in which the intercepts (a) were subsequently re-estimated. This provided alternative hypotheses of strongly density-dependent ($a = 4.154$, $b = -1.377$) and weakly density-dependent reproduction ($a = 1.518$, $b = -0.373$).

Variance of prediction errors.--Using the balance equations and sub-models provided above, predictions of breeding-population size in year $t+1$ depend only on the specification of a regulatory alternative and on an estimate of population size in year t. For the period in which comparisons were possible (1991-96), we were interested in how well these predictions corresponded with observed population sizes. In making these comparisons, we were primarily concerned with how well the bias-corrected balance equations and reproductive and survival sub-models performed. Therefore, we relied on estimates of harvest rates rather than regulations as model inputs.

We estimated the prediction-error variance by setting:

$$e_t = \ln\left(N_t^{obs}\right) - \ln\left(N_t^{pre}\right)$$

$$\text{then assuming} \quad e_t \sim N\left(0, \sigma^2\right)$$

$$\text{and estimating} \quad \hat{\sigma}^2 = \sum_t \left[\ln\left(N_t^{obs}\right) - \ln\left(N_t^{pre}\right)\right]^2 \Big/ n$$

where *obs* and *pre* are observed and predicted population sizes (in millions), respectively, and $n = 6$.

Variance estimates were similar regardless of whether we assumed that the bias was in reproductive rates or in survival, or whether we assumed that reproduction was strongly or weakly density-dependent. Thus, we averaged variance estimates to provide a final estimate of $\sigma^2 = 0.006$, which is equivalent to a coefficient of variation (*CV*) of 8.0%. We were concerned, however, about the small number of years available for estimating this variance. Therefore, we estimated an 80% confidence interval for σ^2 based on a Chi-squared distribution and used the upper limit for $\sigma^2 = 0.018$ (i.e., *CV* = 14.5%) to express the additional uncertainty about the magnitude of prediction errors attributable to potentially important environmental effects not expressed by the models.

Model implications.--Model-specific regulatory strategies based on the hypothesis of weakly density-dependent reproduction are considerably more conservative than those based on the hypothesis of strongly density-dependent reproduction. The three models with weakly density-dependent reproduction suggest a carrying capacity (i.e., average population size in the absence of harvest) >2.0 million mallards, and prescribe extremely restrictive regulations for population size <1.0 million. The three models with strongly density-dependent reproduction suggest a carrying capacity of about 1.5 million mallards, and prescribe liberal regulations for population sizes >300 thousand. Optimal regulatory strategies are relatively insensitive to whether models include a bias correction or not. All model-specific regulatory strategies are "knife-edged," meaning that large differences in the optimal regulatory choice can be precipitated by only small changes in breeding-population size. This result is at least partially due to the small differences in predicted harvest rates among the current regulatory alternatives (see the section on Regulatory Alternatives later in this report).

Model weights.--We calculated weights for the alternative models of eastern mallard population dynamics based on an assumption of equal model weights in 1996 (the last year data was used to develop most model components) and on predictions of year-specific harvest rates. There is no single model that is clearly favored over the others at the end of the time frame, although the three models with strongly density-dependent reproduction currently account for 72% of the total model weight. The reader is warned, however, that (unlike midcontinent mallards) model weights for eastern mallards are still based on predicted rather than empirical harvest rates. Extant model weights could change substantially if and when historic estimates of harvest rates become available.

Table 4. Model-specific predictions and weights for eastern mallards (BnRw = no bias-correction and weakly density-dependent reproduction, BnRs = no bias-correction and strongly density-dependent reproduction, BsRw = bias-corrected survival rates and weakly density-dependent reproduction, BsRs = bias-corrected survival rates and strongly density-dependent reproduction, BrRw = bias-corrected reproductive rates and weakly density-dependent reproduction, and BrRs = bias-corrected reproductive rates and strongly density-dependent reproduction). Model weights were assumed to be equal in 1996.

Year	Bpop(t)[a]	Rate(t)[b]		Model						Observed bpop(t+1)[a]
				BnRw	BnRs	BsRw	BsRs	BrRw	BrRs	
1996	1.1315	0.1510	predicted bpop(t+1):	1.2577	1.1791	1.0511	0.9854	1.0625	1.0074	1.0072
			weight(t+1):	0.0565	0.1100	0.2053	0.2129	0.1996	0.2157	
1997	1.0072	0.1771	predicted bpop(t+1):	1.0853	1.0832	0.9070	0.9053	0.9148	0.9133	1.0389
			weight(t+1):	0.0793	0.1551	0.1840	0.1881	0.1902	0.2032	
1998	1.0389	0.1771	predicted bpop(t+1):	1.1126	1.0923	0.9298	0.9128	0.9388	0.9245	1.0922
			weight(t+1):	0.1308	0.2580	0.1516	0.1307	0.1699	0.1591	
1999	1.0922	0.1771	predicted bpop(t+1):	1.1576	1.1066	0.9674	0.9248	0.9785	0.9427	0.8900
			weight(t+1):	0.0323	0.1146	0.2021	0.2023	0.2144	0.2343	
2000	0.8900	0.1771	predicted bpop(t+1):	0.9815	1.0450	0.8203	0.8733	0.8241	0.8686	1.0077
			weight(t+1):	0.0606	0.2116	0.1226	0.2220	0.1369	0.2463	
2001	1.0077	0.1771	predicted bpop(t+1):	1.0857	1.0833	0.9074	0.9054	0.9152	0.9135	1.0054
			weight(t+1):	0.0653	0.2302	0.1166	0.2086	0.1363	0.2430	
2002	1.0054	0.1871	predicted bpop(t+1):	1.0601	1.0590	0.8860	0.8851	0.8942	0.8934	1.0401
			weight(t+1):	0.0985	0.3474	0.0883	0.1566	0.1116	0.1976	
2003	1.0401	0.1871	predicted bpop(t+1):	1.0893	1.0689	0.9104	0.8933	0.9199	0.9056	1.1107
			weight(t+1):	0.1596	0.5463	0.0494	0.0707	0.0697	0.1043	

[a] Breeding population size (in millions) in the northeastern U.S. (state plot surveys) and eastern Canada (federal survey strata 51-54 and 56) in year t.
[b] Harvest rate of adult-male eastern mallards. Rates are predictions based on models describing the historical relationship between regulations and harvest rate.

Western Mallards

Substantial numbers of mallards occur in the states of the Pacific Flyway (including Alaska), British Columbia, and the Yukon Territory during the breeding season. The distribution of these mallards during fall and winter is centered in the Pacific Flyway (Munro and Kimball 1982). Unfortunately, data-collection programs for understanding and monitoring the dynamics of this mallard stock are highly fragmented in both time and space. This makes it difficult to aggregate monitoring instruments in a way that can be used to reliably model this stock's dynamics and, thus, to establish criteria for regulatory decision-making under AHM (USFWS 2001). Another complicating factor is that federal survey strata 1-12 in Alaska and the Yukon are within the current geographic bounds of midcontinent mallards. Therefore, the AHM Working Group is continuing its investigations of western mallards and is not prepared to recommend an AHM protocol at this time (see page 21 for further details about the effort to develop an AHM approach for western mallards).

HARVEST-MANAGEMENT OBJECTIVES

The basic harvest-management objective for midcontinent mallards is to maximize cumulative harvest over the long term, which inherently requires perpetuation of a viable population. Moreover, this objective is constrained to avoid regulations that could be expected to result in a subsequent population size below the goal of the North American Waterfowl Management Plan (NAWMP) (Fig. 2). According to this constraint, the value of harvest decreases proportionally as the difference between the goal and expected population size increases. This balance of harvest and population objectives results in a regulatory strategy that is more conservative than that for maximizing long-term harvest, but more liberal than a strategy to attain the NAWMP goal (regardless of effects on hunting opportunity). The current objective uses a population goal of 8.8 million mallards, which is based on 8.2 million mallards in the traditional survey area (from the 1998 update of the NAWMP) and a goal of 0.6 million for the combined states of Minnesota, Wisconsin, and Michigan.

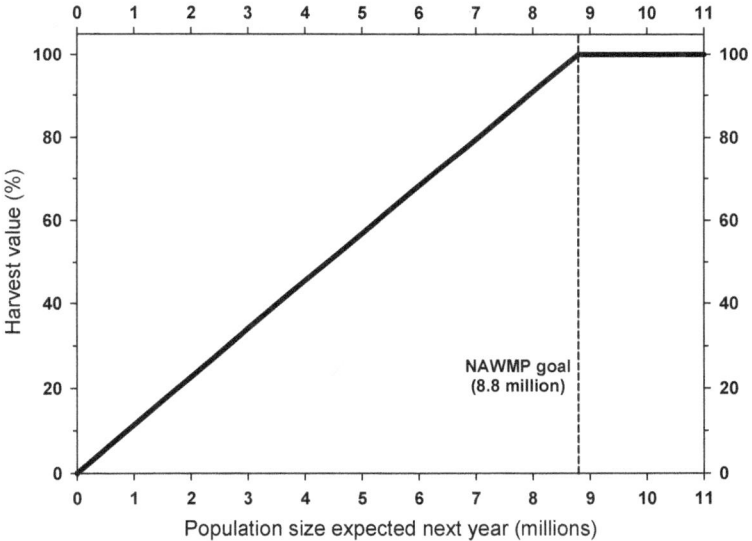

Fig. 2. The relative value of midcontinent mallard harvest, expressed as a function of breeding-population size expected in the subsequent year.

For eastern mallards, there is no NAWMP goal or other established target for desired population size. Accordingly, the management objective for eastern mallards is simply to maximize long-term cumulative (i.e., sustainable) harvest.

REGULATORY ALTERNATIVES

Evolution of Alternatives

When AHM was first implemented in 1995, three regulatory alternatives characterized as liberal, moderate, and restrictive were defined based on regulations used during 1979-84, 1985-87, and 1988-93, respectively. These regulatory alternatives also were considered for the 1996 hunting season. In 1997, the regulatory alternatives were modified to include: (1) the addition of a very-restrictive alternative; (2) additional days and a higher duck bag limit in the moderate and liberal alternatives; and (3) an increase in the bag limit of hen mallards in the moderate and liberal alternatives. In 2002 the USFWS further modified the moderate and liberal alternatives to include extensions of approximately one week in both the opening and closing framework dates.

In 2003 the very-restrictive alternative was eliminated at the request of the Flyway Councils. Expected harvest rates under the very-restrictive alternative did not differ significantly from those under the restrictive alternative, and the very-restrictive alternative was expected to be prescribed for ≤5% of all hunting seasons. Also, at the request of the Flyway Councils the USFWS agreed to exclude closed duck-hunting seasons from the AHM protocol when the breeding-population size of midcontinent mallards is ≥5.5 million (traditional survey area plus the Great Lakes region). Based on our assessment, closed hunting seasons do not appear to be necessary from the perspective of sustainable harvesting when the midcontinent mallard population exceeds this level. The impact of maintaining open seasons above this level also appears to be negligible for other midcontinent duck species (scaup, gadwall, wigeon, green-winged teal, blue-winged teal, shoveler, pintail, redhead, and canvasbacks), as based on population models developed by Johnson (2003). However, complete or partial season-closures for particular species or populations could still be deemed necessary in some situations regardless of the status of midcontinent mallards.

Table 5. Regulatory alternatives for the 2004 duck-hunting season.

Regulation	Flyway			
	Atlantic[a]	Mississippi	Central[b]	Pacific[c]
Shooting hours	one-half hour before sunrise to sunset			
Framework dates				
Restrictive	Oct 1 - Jan 20	Saturday nearest Oct 1 - Sunday nearest Jan 20		
Moderate and Liberal	Saturday nearest Sep 24 - last Sunday in Jan			
Season length (days)				
Restrictive	30	30	39	60
Moderate	45	45	60	86
Liberal	60	60	74	107
Bag limit (total / mallard / female mallard)				
Restrictive	3 / 3 / 1	3 / 2 / 1	3 / 3 / 1	4 / 3 / 1
Moderate	6 / 4 / 2	6 / 4 / 1	6 / 5 / 1	7 / 5 / 2
Liberal	6 / 4 / 2	6 / 4 / 2	6 / 5 / 2	7 / 7 / 2

[a] The states of Maine, Massachusetts, Connecticut, Pennsylvania, New Jersey, Maryland, Delaware, West Virginia, Virginia, and North Carolina are permitted to exclude Sundays, which are closed to hunting, from their total allotment of season days.
[b] The High Plains Mallard Management Unit is allowed 8, 12, 23, and 23 extra days in the restrictive, moderate, and liberal alternatives, respectively.
[c] The Columbia Basin Mallard Management Unit is allowed seven extra days in the restrictive, and moderate alternatives.

Regulation-Specific Harvest Rates

Initially, harvest rates of mallards associated with each of the open-season regulatory alternatives were predicted using harvest-rate estimates from 1979-84, which were adjusted to reflect current hunter numbers and contemporary specifications of season lengths and bag limits. In the case of closed seasons in the U.S., we assumed rates of harvest would be similar to those observed in Canada during 1988-93, which was a period of restrictive regulations both in Canada and the U.S. All harvest-rate predictions were based only in part on band-recovery data, and relied heavily on models of hunting effort and success derived from hunter surveys (USFWS 2002: Appendix C). As such, these predictions had large sampling variances and their accuracy was uncertain.

In 2002 we began relying on Bayesian statistical methods for improving regulation-specific predictions of harvest rates, including predictions of the effects of framework-date extensions. Essentially, the idea is to use existing ("prior") information to develop initial harvest-rate predictions (as above), to make regulatory decisions based on those predictions, and then to observe realized harvest rates. Those observed harvest rates, in turn, are treated as new sources of information for calculating updated ("posterior") predictions. Bayesian methods are attractive because they provide a quantitative and formal, yet intuitive, approach to adaptive management.

For midcontinent mallards, we have empirical estimates of harvest rate from the recent period of liberal hunting regulations (1998-2003). The Bayesian methods thus allow us to combine these estimates with our prior predictions to provide updated estimates of harvest rates expected under the liberal regulatory alternative. Moreover, in the absence of experience (so far) with the restrictive and moderate regulatory alternatives, we reasoned that our initial predictions of harvest rates associated with those alternatives should be re-scaled based on a comparison of predicted and observed harvest rates under the liberal regulatory alternative. In other words, if observed harvest rates under the liberal alternative were 10% less than predicted, then we might also expect that the mean harvest rate under the moderate alternative would be 10% less than predicted. The appropriate scaling factors currently are based exclusively on prior beliefs about differences in mean harvest rate among regulatory alternatives, but they will be updated once we have experience with something other than the liberal alternative. A detailed description of the analytical framework for modeling midcontinent mallard harvest rates is provided in Appendix B.

Our models of regulation-specific harvest rates also allow for the marginal effect of framework-date extensions in the moderate and liberal alternatives. A previous analysis by the USFWS (2000b) suggested that implementation of framework-date extensions might be expected to increase the harvest rate of midcontinent mallards by about 15%, or in absolute terms by about 0.02 (SD = 0.01) (i.e., our "prior" belief). Based on the observed harvest rate during the 2002 and 2003 hunting seasons, the updated ("posterior") estimate of the marginal change in harvest rate attributable to the framework-date extension is 0.0129 (SD = 0.0088). Therefore, the estimated effect of the framework-date extension has been to increase harvest rate of midcontinent mallards by about 11% over what would otherwise be expected in the liberal alternative. However, the reader is strongly cautioned that reliable inference about the marginal effect of framework-date extensions ultimately depends on a rigorous experimental design (including controls and random application of treatments); currently there are no plans to conduct such an experiment.

Current predictions of harvest rates of adult-male midcontinent mallards associated with each of the regulatory alternatives are provided in Table 6 and Fig. 3. Predictions of harvest rates for the other age-sex cohorts are based on the historical ratios of cohort-specific harvest rates to adult-male rates (Runge et al. 2002). These ratios are considered fixed at their long-term averages and are 1.5407, 0.7191, and 1.1175 for young males, adult females, and young females, respectively. We continued to make the simplifying assumption that the harvest rates of midcontinent mallards depend solely on the regulatory choice in the western three Flyways. This appears to be a reasonable assumption given the the small proportion of midcontinent mallards wintering in the Atlantic Flyway (Munro and Kimball 1982), and harvest-rate predictions that suggest a minimal effect of Atlantic Flyway regulations (USFWS 2000a). Under this assumption, the optimal regulatory strategy for the western three Flyways can be derived by ignoring the harvest regulations imposed in the Atlantic Flyway.

For eastern mallards, predictions of harvest rates continue to depend exclusively on historical ("prior") information because more contemporary estimates of harvest rate are not yet available. Thus, we continue to rely on the original predictions of regulation-specific harvest rates and the marginal effect of the framework-date extension (USFWS 2002). However, ongoing band-reporting-rate studies in eastern Canada and the Atlantic Flyway eventually will permit us to update the predictions of eastern-mallard harvest rates in the same fashion as that for midcontinent mallards.

In contrast to midcontinent mallards, harvest rates of eastern mallards appear to depend significantly on regulations beyond the principal Flyway of harvest (USFWS 2000a). Therefore, predictions of harvest rates cannot be based solely on the regulation in the Atlantic Flyway. To avoid making the regulatory choice in the Atlantic Flyway conditional on regulations elsewhere, we inflated the variance of predicted harvest rates of eastern mallards to account for "uncontrolled" changes in regulations in the three western Flyways (Johnson et al. 2002a). Like midcontinent mallards, harvest rates of age and sex cohorts other than adult male mallards are based on constant rates of differential vulnerability as derived from band-recovery data. For eastern mallards, these constants are 1.153, 1.331, and 1.509 for adult females, young males, and young females, respectively (Johnson et al. 2002a). Regulation-specific predictions of harvest rates of adult-male eastern mallards are provided in Table 7 and Fig. 4.

Table 6. Posterior predictions of harvest rates of adult-male midcontinent mallards with application of the 2004 regulatory alternatives in the three western Flyways.

Regulatory alternative	Mean	SD
Closed (U.S.)	0.0088	0.0019
Restrictive	0.0598	0.0129
Moderate	0.1124	0.0217
Liberal	0.1300	0.0225

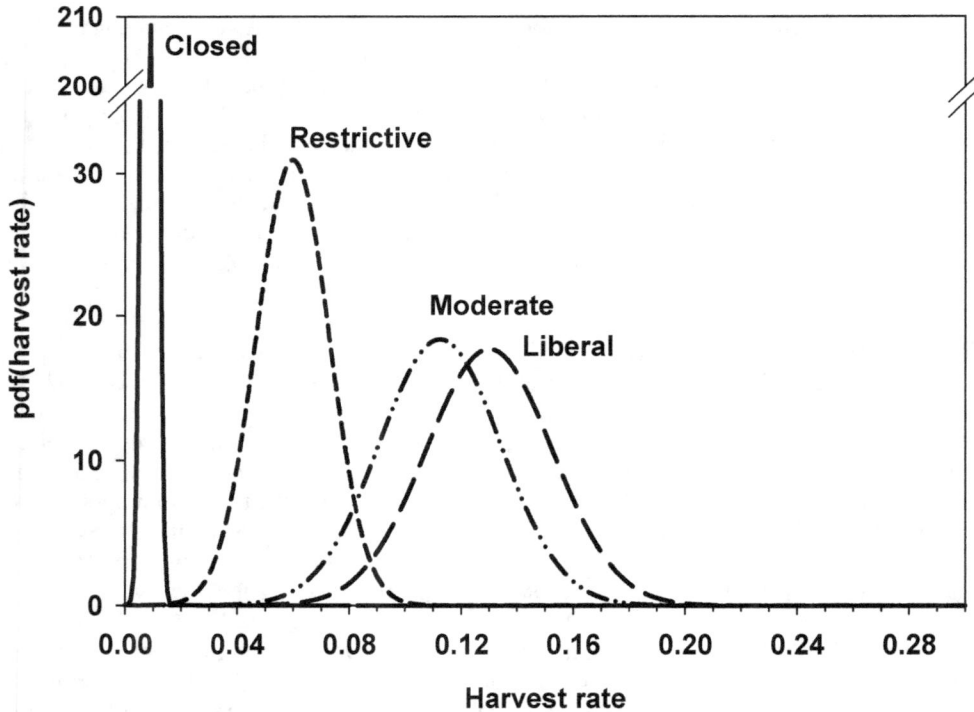

Fig. 3. Posterior probability density functions (pdf) of harvest rates of adult-male midcontinent mallards with application of the 2004 regulatory alternatives in the three western Flyways.

Table 7. Posterior predictions of harvest rates of adult-male eastern mallards with application of the 2004 regulatory alternatives in the Atlantic Flyway.

Regulatory alternative	Mean	SD
Closed (U.S.)	0.0800	0.0240
Restrictive	0.1352	0.0406
Moderate	0.1725	0.0498
Liberal	0.1871	0.0540

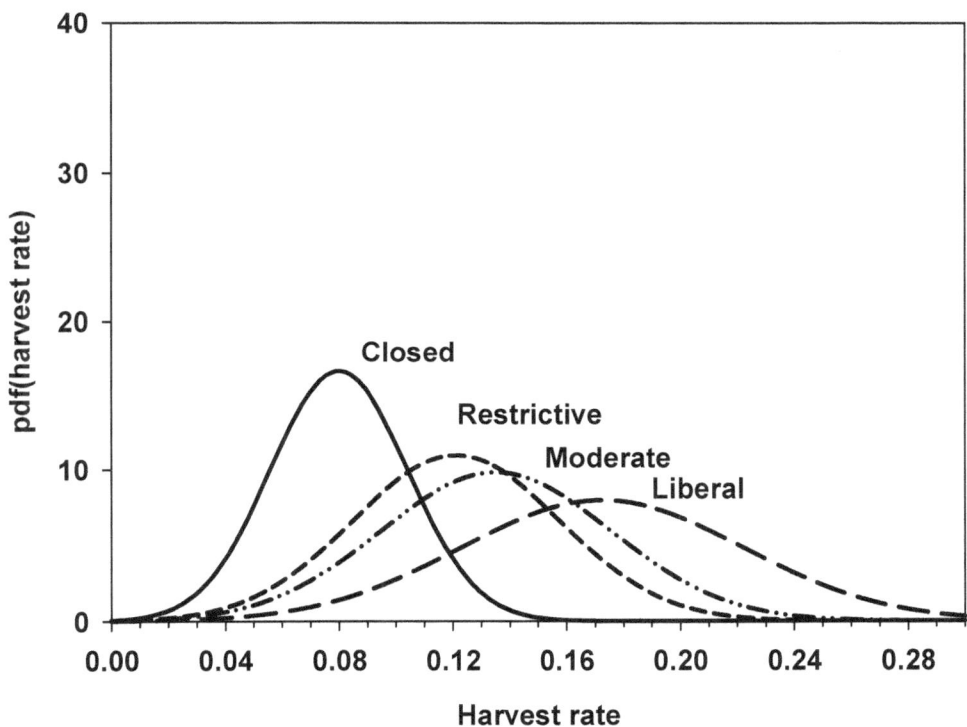

Fig. 4. Posterior probability density functions (pdf) of harvest rates of adult-male eastern mallards with application of the 2004 regulatory alternatives in the Atlantic Flyway.

OPTIMAL REGULATORY STRATEGIES

We calculated optimal regulatory strategies using stochastic dynamic programming (Lubow 1995, Johnson and Williams 1999). For the three western Flyways, we based this optimization on: (1) the 2004 regulatory alternatives, including the closed-season constraint; (2) current population models and associated weights for midcontinent mallards; and (3) the dual objectives of maximizing long-term cumulative harvest and achieving a population goal of 8.8 million midcontinent mallards. The resulting regulatory strategy (Table 8) is similar to that used last year.

Assuming that regulatory choices adhered to this strategy (and that current model weights accurately reflect population dynamics), breeding-population size and harvest value (i.e., annual harvest, devalued when subsequent population size <8.8 million) would be expected to average 7.34 million (SD = 1.76) and 1.06 million (SD = 0.76), respectively. Note that prescriptions for closed seasons in this strategy represent resource conditions that are insufficient to support one of the current regulatory alternatives, given current harvest-management objectives and constraints. However, closed seasons under all of these conditions are not necessarily required for long-term resource protection, and simply reflect the NAWMP population goal and the nature of the current regulatory alternatives.

Based on an observed population size of 8.36 million midcontinent mallards (traditional surveys plus MN, MI, and WI) and 2.51 million ponds in Prairie Canada, the optimal regulatory choice for the Pacific, Central, and Mississippi Flyways in 2004 is the liberal alternative.

Table 8. Optimal regulatory strategy[a] for the three western Flyways for the 2004 hunting season. This strategy is based on current regulatory alternatives (including the closed-season constraint), on current midcontinent-mallard models and weights, and on the dual objectives of maximizing long-term cumulative harvest and achieving a population goal of 8.8 million mallards. The shaded cell indicates the regulatory prescription for 2004.

Bpop[b]	Ponds[c]									
	1.5	2.0	2.5	3.0	3.5	4.0	4.5	5.0	5.5	6.0
≤5.25	C	C	C	C	C	C	C	C	C	C
5.50-6.25	R	R	R	R	R	R	R	R	R	R
6.50	R	R	R	R	R	R	R	R	R	M
6.75	R	R	R	R	R	R	R	M	M	L
7.00	R	R	R	R	R	M	M	M	L	L
7.25	R	R	R	M	M	M	L	L	L	L
7.50	R	R	M	M	L	L	L	L	L	L
7.75	R	M	M	L	L	L	L	L	L	L
8.00	M	M	L	L	L	L	L	L	L	L
8.25	M	L	L	L	L	L	L	L	L	L
≥8.5	L	L	L	L	L	L	L	L	L	L

[a] C = closed season, R = restrictive, M = moderate, L = liberal.
[b] Mallard breeding population size (in millions) in the traditional survey area (survey strata 1-18, 20-50, 75-77) and Michigan, Minnesota, and Wisconsin.
[c] Ponds (in millions) in Prairie Canada in May.

We calculated an optimal regulatory strategy for the Atlantic Flyway based on: (1) the 2004 regulatory alternatives; (2) current population models and associated weights for eastern mallards; and (3) an objective to maximize long-term cumulative harvest. The resulting strategy suggests liberal regulations for all population sizes of record, and is characterized by a lack of intermediate regulations (Table 9). The strategy exhibits this behavior in part because of the small differences in harvest rate among regulatory alternatives (Fig. 4).

Table 9. Optimal regulatory strategy[a] for the Atlantic Flyway for the 2004 hunting season. This strategy is based on current regulatory alternatives, on current eastern-mallard models and weights, and on an objective to maximize long-term cumulative harvest. The shaded cell indicates the regulatory prescription for 2004.

Mallards[b]	Regulation
≤175	C
200	R
225	M
≥250	L

[a] C = closed season, R = restrictive, M = moderate, and L = liberal.
[b] Estimated number of mallards in eastern Canada (survey strata 51-54, 56) and the northeastern U.S. (state plot surveys), in thousands.

We simulated the use of the regulatory strategy in Table 9 to determine expected performance characteristics. Assuming that harvest management adhered to this strategy (and that current model weights accurately reflect population dynamics), the annual breeding-population size and harvest would be expected to average 1.01 million (SD = 0.18) and 557 thousand (SD = 147), respectively.

Based on a breeding population size of 1.11 million mallards, the optimal regulatory choice for the Atlantic Flyway in 2004 is the liberal alternative.

Ongoing Development of AHM

Policy Issues

Last year the International Association of Fish and Wildlife Agencies convened a task force comprised of recognized leaders in waterfowl management to help address policy questions related to future application of AHM. These policy questions involve the specification of harvest-management objectives, the role (if any) of the NAWMP population objectives in harvest management, specification of the set of regulatory alternatives, and various regulatory approaches for managing the harvest of species other than mallards. This task force is working closely with the Flyway Councils, the USFWS, the AHM Working Group, and other interested parties and is dedicated to developing as much consensus as possible on the issues at hand. For more information about the task force, including its most recent recommendations, visit http://migratorybirds.fws.gov/mgmt/ahm/taskforce/taskforce.htm.

Efforts to Expand the Scope of AHM

Western mallards.--Efforts to understand the population dynamics of western mallards have been underway for several years. In support of this effort, the Pacific Flyway States and the USFWS have worked cooperatively to improve survey and banding programs throughout the breeding range of western mallards. In addition, two assessment projects have been cooperatively funded:

(1) In 1998, funding was provided to the New York Cooperative Fish and Wildlife Research Unit to compile survey, banding, and harvest data, and to develop models describing the population dynamics of western mallards. A final report, which was issued in 1999, provided estimates of mortality and reproductive rates for western mallards, as well as a preliminary assessment of how these rates might vary as a function of environmental conditions and harvest. This project was cooperatively funded by the USFWS ($15,000), Ducks Unlimited ($15,000), the Pacific Flyway Council ($10,000), the California Dept. of Fish and Game ($10,000), and California Waterfowl Association ($10,000) (total = $60,000). (An additional $60,000 was provided concurrently by these same partners to advance AHM for pintails.)

21

(2) After completion of the first cooperative assessment project, the AHM Working Group identified a number of technical concerns with the initial effort to model population dynamics. In January 2003, the University of Nevada - Reno hired a post-doctoral fellow to address these concerns. This effort is being cooperatively funded by the Pacific Flyway Council ($20,000), the State of Oregon ($20,000), and the USFWS ($17,000) (total = $57,000).

In May 2004, the USFWS received a draft of the final report from the University of Nevada for review. The report documents an attempt to integrate several sources of data to model variation in western-mallard abundance as a function of survival and reproductive processes. The approach used is similar to that used successfully for both midcontinent (Runge et al. 2002) and eastern (Johnson et al. 2002) mallards. The USFWS currently is working with the contractor and other project partners to complete a final report. At this time, however, the USFWS remains concerned:

(1)   that extant data and on-going monitoring programs may be insufficient to reliably discern patterns of abundance and demographic rates across the breeding range of western mallards;
(2)   that a reliable method for estimating reproductive rates has not yet been convincingly demonstrated; and
(3)   that an assumption of a closed population (i.e., immigration and emigration are ignored) may be inappropriate, particularly for mallards breeding in Alaska.

Assuming these concerns can be addressed, additional efforts will be necessary:

(1)   to assess the relationship between hunting regulations and the harvest rates of western mallards;
(2)   to explore and agree on appropriate harvest-management objectives for western mallards; and
(3)   to integrate western and midcontinent mallard AHM in a way that appropriately recognizes the mixing of these two stocks during the hunting season.

The USFWS and the USGS are continuing work on these topics.

Northern pintails.--The development of an AHM strategy for northern pintails has been challenging on both technical and political levels. As we move beyond mallards to develop more quantitative harvest strategies for other species, we face two fundamental difficulties: greater uncertainty about the biology because monitoring data are sparser, and the political challenge of identifying management objectives and regulatory actions for multiple stocks.

For pintails, there continue to be three technical issues that are impeding development of an AHM strategy:

(1) There is evidence of a temporal trend in reproductive rates, presumably due to habitat changes in the western Canadian prairies. In the past, reproduction was strongly influenced by the latitude of the breeding population. In years when the prairies were wet and pintails settled in the southern part of their breeding range, reproductive success was high; in years when pintails overflew the prairies, reproduction was low. However, this effect appears to have disappeared over time, so that now even when the prairies are wet and pintails settle there, reproductive success is not very high. From a decision-making perspective this presents a challenge because of uncertainty about whether (and to what extent) the trend in the reproductive process will continue in the future.

(2) There are several apparent biases in the monitoring programs for pintails, but we do not yet know their cause or how to compensate for them. When combined into a "balance equation," estimates of survival and reproductive rates over-predict the growth rate of the population. Moreover, the magnitude of the over-prediction is related to where the birds settle. That is, when pintail overfly the prairies, population estimates appear to be biased low. The first type of bias (balance-equation bias) is also seen in midcontinent and eastern mallards, and we have successfully developed remedial measures. But we do not yet have an acceptable means to correct for the over-flight bias.

(3) It will be difficult to develop a predictive model for harvest rate as a function of regulations. This is a key component in AHM because it is the link between the management action and the effect on the population. Estimates for pintail harvest rates have wide confidence intervals because of the small number of birds that are banded and recovered each year. Because of the attendant large sampling errors, it will be difficult to discern the extent to which changes in regulations affect changes in harvest rate.

To date, the USFWS has been unable to assemble the fiscal and personnel resources necessary to address these issues in the face of competing priorities. This problem can be overcome eventually, but there are still three remaining impediments, each of which is a human-dimensions question that must be answered in the political arena:

(1) How will decisions about pintail harvest interact with decisions about mallard harvest? What regulatory structure is desired: independent regulations for each species, a common season length but separate bag limits, or the same regulations? If a common season length is desired, should the season be set by mallard status and the pintail bag set conditionally, or should the regulations for the two species be jointly optimized?

(2) What are the objectives for pintail management? There are many possible objectives, including to maximize harvest, to provide incentive for winter habitat conservation, to provide consistent hunting opportunity, and to avoid closed seasons. How are these objectives to be balanced against one another, and how are they to be balanced against management objectives for mallards and other species?

(3) How much should managers forego harvest opportunity to promote recovery of the pintail population? There is strong consensus that the decline in the pintail population is due to habitat degradation rather than harvest. Nevertheless, harvest levels could influence the speed and extent of population recovery.

Black ducks.–In 1999 a working group (BDAHMWG) was formed to investigate how the U.S. and Canada might cooperate in an adaptive approach to the management of black duck harvests. The BDAHMWG was formed by, and provides technical advice to, a Black Duck International Harvest Strategy Committee (HSC). The HSC is comprised of seven representatives from the USFWS, the CWS, and the Atlantic and Mississippi Flyway Councils. The BDAHMWG includes the seven members of the HSC along with others who are involved in the technical aspects of the effort. AHM for black ducks is viewed as a means of dealing with (rather than resolving) uncertainties in population dynamics, particularly those concerning the role of mallard competition and sport harvest in the long-term decline in black duck abundance.

Working under contract, the Cooperative Fish and Wildlife Research Unit in Georgia has been leading the technical effort to develop an international AHM framework for black ducks. The effort has successfully produced models of the continental black duck population that recognize four alternative biological hypotheses (presence or absence of a mallard effect on reproduction, additive or compensatory hunting mortality) and that explicitly account for an apparent bias in estimates of survival and reproductive rates (Conroy et al. 2002). The developing AHM framework also includes: (a) breeding-population goals; (b) parity in U.S. and Canadian harvests; and (c) possible regulatory alternatives. An extension of this framework to three breeding stocks and six harvest areas (three in eastern Canada, two in the Atlantic Flyway, and the Mississippi Flyway) also is being explored. A final report from the Georgia Cooperative Fish and Wildlife Research Unit is expected this summer. For more information about the effort to develop an AHM approach to black ducks visit http://coopunit.forestry.uga.edu/blackduck/.

Atlantic Population of Canada geese.–The size of the Atlantic Population (AP) of Canada geese (*Branta canadensis*) declined significantly in the 1980s and early 1990s (Hestbeck 1995, Hestbeck and Malecki 1989). Sport-hunting seasons for this population were closed in the U.S. from the fall of 1995 to the winter of 1999. Hunting seasons were subsequently reinstated, but are currently at restrictive to moderate levels in the U.S. Continuation of sport hunting for AP Canada geese and maintenance of the population within desired bounds are contingent upon effective harvest management and monitoring programs. Effective management will depend on tradeoffs among multiple objectives, and must be accomplished with incomplete knowledge of the system and in the presence of environmental variation, partial system control, and partial system observability.

Development of an AHM protocol for AP Canada geese will require extending current AHM approaches to account for fundamental differences in the demography and management of ducks and geese. To date, applications of adaptive management to waterfowl harvesting have relied on simple scalar population models (Johnson et al. 1997). Such scalar models assume all individuals in the population have similar responses to environmental stressors. By contrast, goose populations have significant age structure as a result of relatively high survival rates and age-dependent productivity (Raveling 1981, Raveling et al. 2000). Previous investigations have shown that optimal harvests of goose populations are conditional on the age-structure of the population and on age-specific differences in harvest vulnerability (Evan Cooch, Cornell University, pers. comm.).

The Atlantic Flyway Council, the USGS, Cornell University, the USFWS, and the CWS are now collaborating to develop an AHM protocol for the sport harvest of AP Canada geese. The project objectives are:

(1)   to explore the general implications of age structure, non-equilibrium population dynamics, and population momentum for managing the sport harvest of geese;

(2)   to develop a set of models describing population and harvest dynamics for geese and parameterize these models using data specific to AP Canada geese, or to other populations comprised principally of *B. canadensis interior*;

(3)   to identify key uncertainties in population or harvest dynamics (i.e., those to which optimal harvest policies are sensitive); and

(4)   to derive adaptive policies specifying optimal state-specific harvest rates, and demonstrate the expected performance of these policies.

An analytical framework for an AHM program for AP Canada geese was developed last autumn (for more information see http://migratorybirds.fws.gov/reports/ahm03/apcg_report1_r6.pdf). Cooperators are now exploring in more detail the general problem of harvest optimization for age-structured populations, and have begun to parameterize a set of models describing the dynamics of AP Canada geese. A final project report is expected in the winter of 2004-05.

Application of AHM Concepts to Stocks of Concern

In addition to ongoing efforts to develop full-featured AHM protocols for a number of waterfowl stocks, the USFWS is striving to apply the principles and tools of AHM to improve decision-making for several stocks of special concern. We here report on two such efforts in which significant progress has been made since last year.

Black Ducks

Management of American black ducks (*Anas rubripes*) has long been hampered by a lack of understanding regarding the factors affecting annual abundance. This has resulted in disagreements among stakeholders about whether to use hunting regulations to arrest the large-scale decline of black ducks, and ultimately how to provide sustainable hunting opportunities. We began working with the Atlantic Flyway Council and others to develop assessment procedures that could be used to inform black duck harvest management in the United States until such time that an international strategy is agreed upon and implemented. These procedures are intended to help the USFWS assess the biological implications of any proposed changes to hunting regulations, as well as complement the ongoing effort to develop an international program for the adaptive management of black duck harvests.

Development of a useful assessment protocol requires the specification of harvest management objectives, models of black duck population dynamics, and acceptable regulatory alternatives:

Harvest-management objectives.—The BDAHMWG supports a basic objective of maximizing long-term cumulative (i.e., sustainable) harvest, possibly subject to two constraints. First, there is general agreement that any harvest strategy should not disrupt the tradition of approximate parity in harvest between the U.S. and Canada. Second, a harvest strategy that helps maintain population size above some numeric goal has wide appeal, although there is not yet consensus on the magnitude of the goal, nor on the appropriate tradeoff between harvest and the goal as the population falls below goal. For the purposes of these assessment procedures, we calculated optimal harvest strategies for both an objective to maximize sustainable harvest and an objective that also includes the original NAWMP goal of 385 thousand black ducks in the midwinter inventory. The NAWMP-goal constraint was implemented in the same fashion as that used for midcontinent mallards (see page 15). Approximate harvest parity was achieved by constraining harvest rates to be the same in Canada and the U.S. (i.e., the two countries were allowed only an equal proportion of the birds available to them). Other ways to impose a parity constraint are also being investigated.

Models of population dynamics.—Spatially stratified population models are under development by the BDAHMWG but are not yet ready for application. Therefore, these assessment procedures rely on the black duck population models described by Conroy et al. (2002). These models describe a single continental population of black ducks, and were parameterized using midwinter inventories to index population size. There are eight models, based on combinations of two reproductive

24

hypotheses (mallard competition vs. no mallard competition), two survival hypotheses (density-dependent vs. density-independent mortality), and two hypotheses regarding the positive bias in predictions of population size (bias is in survival-rate estimates vs. bias is in reproductive-rate estimates). Because of the existence of competing models of population dynamics, the assessment procedures rely on model averaging, using the most recent empirical determination of model weights.

Four of the population models suggest that black duck reproductive rates decline with increasing numbers of sympatric mallards. Therefore, it was necessary to include a dynamic model of mallard population size. We used a simple model, in which annual growth rates were randomly drawn from the empirical distribution of observed growth rates. We imposed lower and upper bounds of 100 thousand and 1 million, respectively, to maintain the mallard population within a realistic range. This mallard model should be considered a place-holder for the more sophisticated models that ultimately will be necessary for an adaptive management strategy.

Regulatory alternatives.—Ultimately, the purpose of these assessment procedures is to guide the setting of hunting regulations in the Mississippi and Atlantic Flyways, either separately or jointly. Therefore, the identification and assessment of a U.S. regulatory strategy must involve at a minimum: (a) development of models that describe the relationship between U.S. hunting regulations and harvest rates of black ducks, (b) identification of acceptable regulatory alternatives in the U.S., and (c) an assumption about regulations or rates of harvest in Canada in the absence of a coordinated, international harvest strategy. These elements of the assessment procedure are being developed. In the meantime, we focus here on harvest rates that have been observed in the past and on those that are projected to be optimal (based on various management objectives) for the black duck population as a whole.

Sources of data, the structure of population models, and estimation methods are described in detail by Conroy et al. (2002). To calculate optimal harvest strategies, we used the generalized software for stochastic dynamic programming developed by Lubow (1995). Optimal harvest strategies were those that maximized the long-term cumulative sum of undiscounted, annual harvests, in some cases subject to the constraints described above. For each management objective, we evaluated adult-male harvest rates of 0.0-0.2 (in increments of 0.01), for black duck population sizes of 0-1.5 million (in increments of 50 thousand) and for mallard population sizes of 0-1 million (in increments of 50000). We assumed perfect controllability of harvest rates throughout. In each case we accounted for residual error, specifying the degree to which the (average) population model of black ducks failed to describe observed changes in population size.

To understand general patterns of optimal harvests for a single, continental population of black ducks, we first conducted an equilibrium analysis (Walters 1986). In this case, equilibrium analysis provides the expected relationship between population size and sustainable harvest assuming a constant annual harvest rate, a fixed number of mallards, and constant environmental conditions. While these conditions clearly are unrealistic, equilibrium analysis nonetheless serves to elucidate the harvest dynamics associated with models of population growth. In Fig. 5, we show the sustainable levels of harvest associated with various population sizes of black ducks, for varying levels of sympatric mallards. The figure demonstrates how both black duck population size in the absence of harvest (i.e., where the curves intercept the horizontal axis on the right side of the graph) and the size of the sustainable harvest decrease with increasing number of mallards. For all levels of mallards depicted, the maximum sustainable black duck harvest is achieved at black duck population sizes below the NAWMP goal of 385 thousand wintering black ducks. Therefore, imposition of the NAWMP goal for the wintering population will constrain hunting opportunity from what it would be otherwise.

State-dependent, optimal harvest rates for adult males are depicted in Fig. 6. These harvest strategies account for random fluctuations in mallard abundance and environmental conditions, and prescribe an optimal harvest rate based on the numbers of black ducks and mallards observed each year. As expected, the harvest strategy incorporating the NAWMP goal of 385 thousand black ducks is more conservative than the harvest strategy designed to maximize sustainable harvest.

We also were interested in how these optimal harvest rates compared with observed harvest rates over the period of record. For this comparison we used estimates of adult male harvest rates during 1961-1994 that were provided by Conroy et al. (2002). Empirical estimates of harvest rates for 1995 and later years are unavailable due to uncertain changes in reporting rate associated with the introduction of a toll-free phone number for reporting band recoveries. Therefore, we used the historic relationship between observed harvest rates and a crude index of harvest rate derived from harvest and the midwinter survey index (MWI) [i.e., harvest ÷ (harvest + MWI)] to predict harvest rates for the 1995-2002 hunting seasons. The relationship between the logit-transformed estimate of the harvest rate and the index based on harvest and MWI was reasonably strong (P < 0.01, R^2 = 0.43), and its prediction for the 2002 hunting season was similar to a preliminary estimate derived from recent reward banding. We therefore used the predicted harvest rates for 1995-2002, along with the empirical estimates from 1961-1994, to compare with optimal rates. "Observed" harvest rates tended to correspond fairly well with optimal rates under an objective to maximize harvest, constrained by the NAWMP goal of 385k wintering black ducks (Fig. 7). However, optimal harvest rates under a sole objective to maximize sustainable harvest tended to be higher than those "observed." These results suggest that a judgement about the desirability of effecting changes in black duck harvest rates depends critically on the acceptability of the NAWMP midwinter population goal as a management objective.

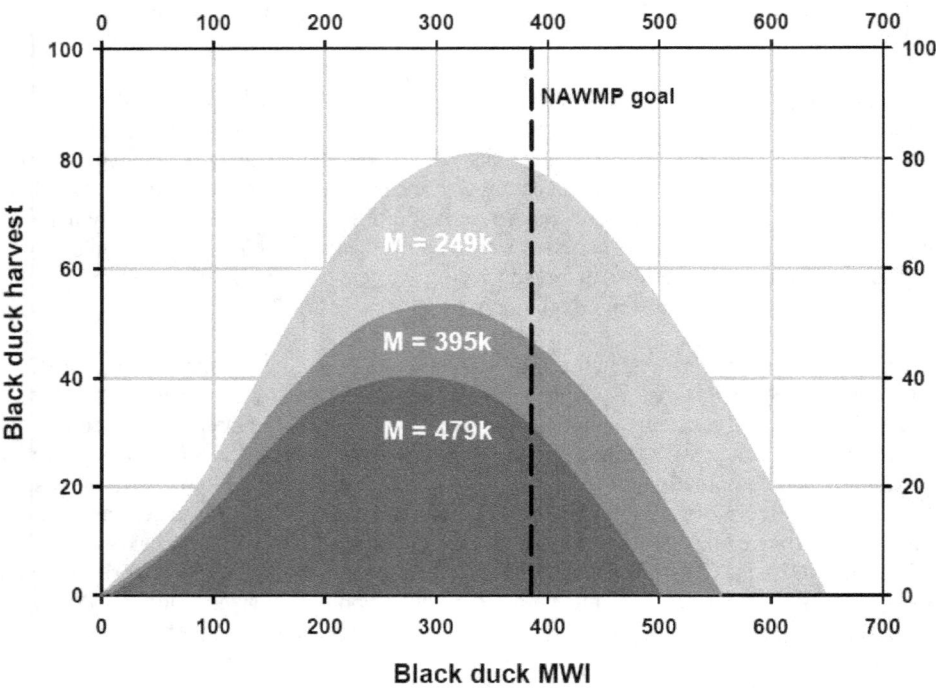

Fig. 5. Equilibrium harvests and population sizes (MWI = midwinter inventory) of black ducks assuming constant harvests, a fixed number of midwinter mallards (M), and constant environmental conditions. The three levels of mallards represent the most recent 10-year average (395k), and the 5% and 95% quantiles during the period 1961-2003. The analysis was based on models and model weights provided by Conroy et al. (2002).

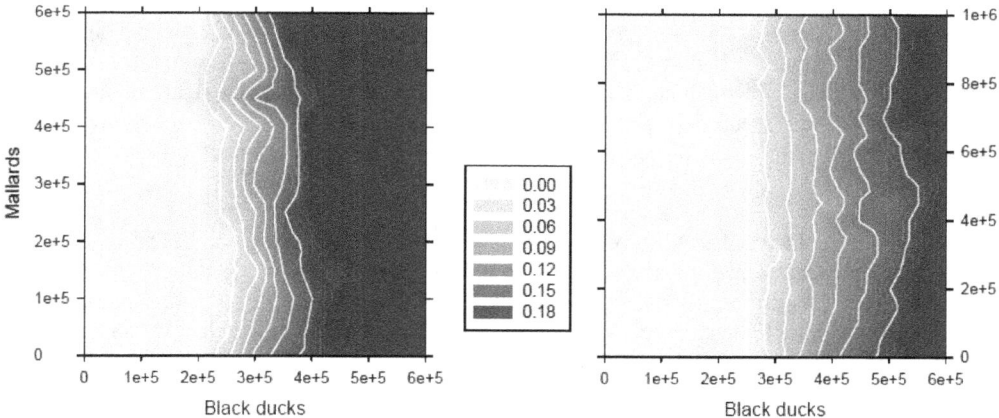

Fig. 6. Optimal harvest rates of adult-male black ducks, conditioned on midwinter inventories of black ducks and mallards. The left graph depicts a strategy to maximize sustainable harvests, while the right graph depicts a strategy that also includes the NAWMP goal of 385 thousand black ducks in the midwinter inventory. These strategies were based on models and model weights provided by Conroy et al. (2002).

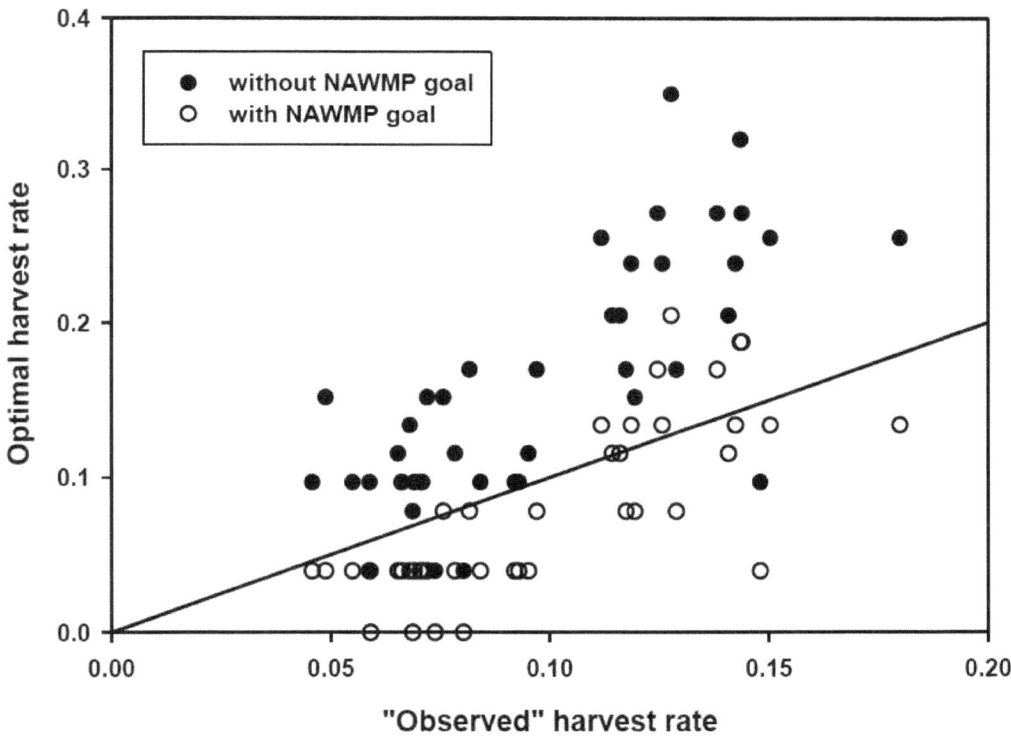

Fig. 7. Optimal harvest rates of adult-male black ducks designed to maximize sustainable harvest (with and without the NAWMP goal as a constraint), compared with "observed" harvest rates during 1961-2002. "Observed" harvest rates include empirical estimates (1961-94) from Conroy et al. (2002) and model-based predictions for 1995-2002 (see text). Optimal harvest rates were based on models and model weights provided by Conroy et al. (2002). Points falling along the diagonal line indicate close correspondence between optimal and observed harvest rates.

Scaup

The persistent status of scaup (*Aythya affinis*, *A. marila*) populations below the NAWMP goal has highlighted the need for a predictive decision-making framework to direct harvest management. However, the development of such a framework is problematic because of the large levels of uncertainty concerning our ability to monitor scaup populations, as well as our incomplete understanding of how scaup populations respond to exploitation. Therefore, we are attempting to develop an assessment framework that balances the limited amount of information available with the desired biological realism of population models.

Population modeling.--We evaluated the utility of using a simple surplus-production population model within a Bayesian estimation framework to represent scaup population dynamics. Under this formulation, population dynamics are modeled with a simple difference equation as opposed to a traditional balance equation that uses sex and age-specific survival and recruitment rates to represent population change. We modified an existing assessment model (Meyer and Millar 1999, Millar and Meyer 2000) for application to the available scaup monitoring information. These data include spring breeding-population estimates from the traditional survey area from 1961 - 2002, harvest estimates from the U.S. (1961 - 2002) and Canada (1974 - 2002), and estimates of hunting effort (total hunter days) in the U.S. from 1961 - 2002. All numbers were taken from the recent review of scaup status (Allen et al. 1999) and USFWS reports (Wilkins and Otto 2003, Martin and Padding 1998, 1999, 2000, 2001, and 2002).

We used a logistic, difference equation (Hilborn and Walters 1992, Quinn and Deriso 1999) to model changes in population size N in year t according to:

$$N_{t+1} = N_t + rN_t(1 - \frac{N_t}{K}) - H_t,$$

where r is the intrinsic rate of population growth, K is the carrying capacity, and H is the total harvest in year t. With this very simple equation, population change is governed by two population parameters. More importantly, the harvest process is explicitly considered in the population model. This is the fundamental connection that provides a linkage between harvest-management decisions and predicted changes in scaup abundance.

Bayesian estimation.--The goal of this assessment work was to develop a framework to represent scaup population dynamics with an ability to predict changes in population sizes with annually updated monitoring information. In order for these predictions to be useful in a management context, decision makers must be able to make probabilistic statements regarding the likelihood of a particular outcome. Therefore, the model requires parameter estimates and realistic representations of their variances. Ideally, an assessment model must be able to not only represent the uncertainty associated with the monitoring information (observation error), but also must account for an incomplete understanding of population dynamics (process error). Therefore, we modified an existing Bayesian estimation framework (Meyer and Millar 1999, Millar and Meyer 2000) that explicitly considers both of these types of uncertainty to estimate scaup population parameters while also providing probability distributions associated with population predictions useful for decision making.

We developed and evaluated a suite of population models that varied in how the model parameters r or K were allowed to vary over time. We considered possible temporal changes in these parameters to account for possible large-scale system changes that may be associated with the decline in scaup abundance. Our initial assessment used a simple random walk to represent possible temporal changes in r or K.

We used Markov Chain Monte Carlo (MCMC) methods to evaluate each posterior distribution using WinBUGS (Spiegelhalter et al. 2003). More details concerning our modeling and estimation approach can be found in a recent progress report (http://migratorybirds.fws.gov/reports/ahm04/scaup.pdf).

Assessment results.--Our models provided surprisingly good explanations of the population and harvest-survey information (Figs. 8 and 9). Crude harvest rates calculated as a product of a "catchability" parameter (q) and the level of observed effort (total hunter days) were variable ranging from 0.0376 to 0.105, and were similar regardless of which model was used. In general, scaup harvest rates tracked population levels from the mid 1960s until the early 1990s. However, the results from this assessment suggest that this relationship may have changed starting in the early 1990s when harvest rates increased, while

28

population sizes continued to decline (Fig. 10). The 2003 breeding-population prediction based on the scaup production model with constant *r* and *K* differed from the observed 2003 breeding population estimate by less than 1.1% (Table 10).

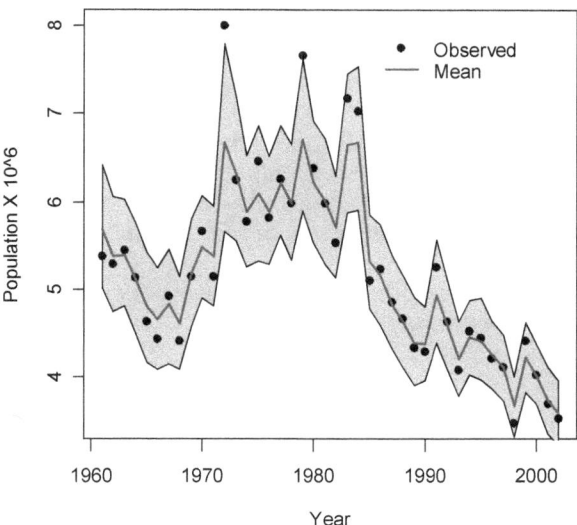

Fig. 8. Posterior estimates of scaup population size (and shaded 95% credibility intervals) from a logistic growth model with constant *r* and *K* (see text) as compared with those observed in the Breeding Population and Habitat Survey.

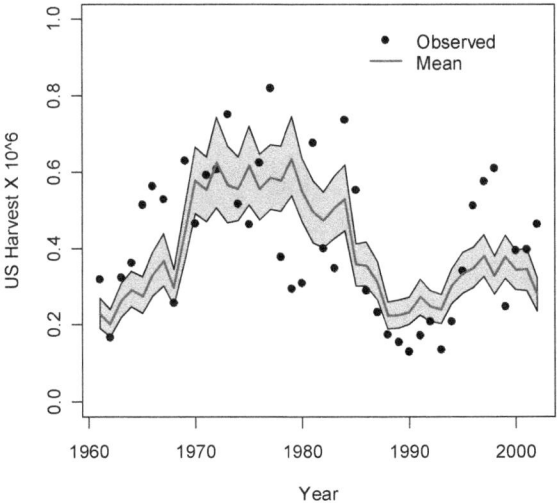

Fig. 9. Posterior estimates of U.S. scaup harvest (and shaded 95% credibility intervals) from a logistic growth model with constant *r* and *K* (see text) as compared with those observed in the Waterfowl Harvest Surveys.

Decision-making application.--A benefit of our modeling approach is the ability to estimate harvest-management parameters (e.g., maximum sustained yield [MSY], population size at MSY, optimal harvest rates). We explored ways in which these management parameters and the results of the scaup assessment could be useful in a decision-making context. We parameterized the logistic, population model with the results of the population assessment, while explicitly accounting for variation in *r* and *K* and the process uncertainty associated with our representation of scaup population dynamics.

Classic MSY harvest theory suffers from a number of shortcomings that limit its usefulness in harvest management. It fails to account for uncontrolled environmental factors that prevent populations from achieving equilibrium, it does not account for potential temporal changes in population parameters (*r* or *K*), nor does it address the inherent uncertainty associated with our ability to describe scaup population changes with the logistic model (process error). To overcome these problems, we used discrete, stochastic dynamic programming (Puterman 1994) to derive a closed-loop harvest strategy. Closed-loop harvest strategies involve a feedback mechanism whereby harvests are adjusted periodically based on observed rather than predicted changes in population size. We used generalized software developed by Lubow (1995) to derive model-specific harvest strategies intended to maximize the long-term cumulative sum of undiscounted, annual harvests.

Using the population model with constant *r* and *K*, the optimal harvest strategy prescribes no harvests for N < 2.75 million. The optimal level of harvest then increases sharply with increases in N, reaching maximum sustainable levels when the population size is about 3.4 million (i.e., *K*/2).

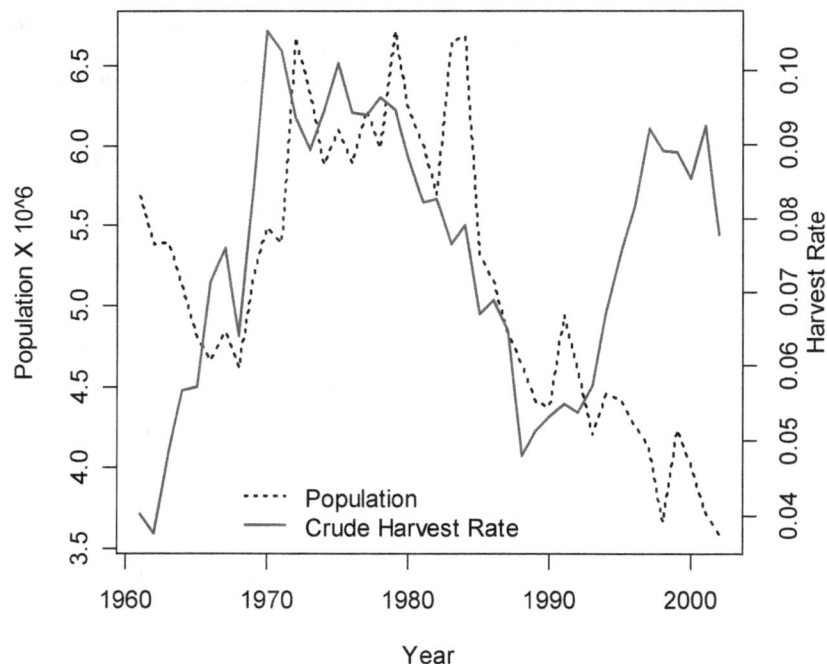

Fig. 10. Estimates of scaup population size and harvest rate as based on a logistic growth model with constant *r* and *K* (see text).

Table 10. Bayesian parameter estimates (posterior means) and 95% credibility intervals (LCI, UCI) for logistic models of scaup population growth, as based on population and harvest data during 1961-2003.

θ	Model M0 Constant r, constant K			Model M1 Varying r, constant K			Model M2 Constant r, varying K		
	Mean	LCI	UCI	Mean	LCI	UCI	Mean	LCI	UCI
r	0.2990	0.1590	0.4845	0.1737[a]	0.0007	0.6183	1.0100	0.3339	1.7670
K	6.8370	5.9790	8.0520	6.5770	6.1260	7.1150	4.2320[a]	3.6060	5.4860
q	0.0062	0.0054	0.0069	0.0063	0.0055	0.0070	0.0063	0.0056	0.0071
$\sigma^2_{process}$	0.0150	0.0080	0.0265	0.0078	0.0018	0.0193	0.0024	0.0004	0.0076
$\sigma^2_{harvest}$	0.0249	0.0156	0.0393	0.0242	0.0153	0.0378	0.0246	0.0156	0.0381
σ^2_{walk}	n/a	n/a	n/a	0.4866	0.0417	2.0810	0.0052	0.0018	0.0116
N_{2003}[b]	3.7740	3.3340	4.2080	3.5100	2.9780	4.3790	3.7000	3.2910	4.1330

[a]Parameter estimates from 2002 as based on the random-walk models.
[b]The breeding population estimate for 2003, as predicted based on population and harvest information from 2002. The observed scaup population size in 2003 was 3.7344 million.

Discussion.--The Bayesian population assessment using the logistic surplus-production model resulted in a reasonable representation of population change based on a limited amount of information. The state-space formulation of Meyer and Millar (1999) provided an efficient estimation framework that realistically accounted for process and observation uncertainty. From a decision-making context, the results of the Bayesian assessment are useful because the probability distributions associated with each estimate permits one to make probabilistic statements regarding changes in population size, as well as characterize the uncertainty surrounding the population and management parameter estimates.

Despite the utility of these analyses, however, we suggest that caution is warranted in using these results for scaup harvest-management purposes. First, application of the fitted models requires that we impart biological meaning to model parameters r and K (i.e., they accurately describe the mechanisms underlying changes in population size). Secondly, we only considered a single functional form of the logistic model. This functional form describes a perfectly symmetric growth curve with an inflection point (i.e., the population size with the highest harvestable surplus) at $K/2$. Non-symmetric growth curves are possible and may be the norm in nature. Fowler (1981) hypothesized that K-selected species may experience the greatest density-dependent effects on growth rate at populations sizes only slightly less than K. If this were true for scaup, we would expect the harvest strategies to be much more conservative than those described in this report. We thus consider the investigation of different functional forms of the logistic model to be a high priority in scaup harvest management.

We believe our results highlight the importance of developing a long-term harvest management strategy for scaup that balances the trade-off between population recovery and harvest opportunity. To develop such a strategy, issues of model selection, management objectives, and ultimately the coupling of regulatory actions with observable harvest responses will have to be addressed. The existing scaup assessment provides a useful first step in the development of a rigorous decision-making framework for a rational, long-term scaup harvest strategy.

LITERATURE CITED

Allen, G. T., D. F. Caithamer, and M. Otto. 1999. A review of the status of greater and lesser scaup in North America. U.S. Dept. Interior, Washington, D. C. 45pp.

Anderson, D. R., and K. P. Burnham. 1976. Population ecology of the mallard. VI. The effect of exploitation on survival. U.S. Fish and Wildlife Service Resource Publication No. 128. 66pp.

Blohm, R. J. 1989. Introduction to harvest - understanding surveys and season setting. Proceedings of the International Waterfowl Symposium 6:118-133.

Blohm, R. J., R. E. Reynolds, J. P. Bladen, J. D. Nichols, J. E. Hines, K. P. Pollock, and R. T. Eberhardt. 1987. Mallard mortality rates on key breeding and wintering areas. Transactions of the North American Wildlife and Natural Resources Conference 52:246-263.

Burnham, K. P., G. C. White, and D. R. Anderson. 1984. Estimating the effect of hunting on annual survival rates of adult mallards. Journal of Wildlife Management 48:350-361.

Conroy, M. J., M. W. Miller, and J. E. Hines. 2002. Identification and synthetic modeling of factors affecting American black duck populations. Wildlife Monographs 150. 64pp.

Fowler. C. W. 1981. Density dependence as related to life history strategy. Ecology 62:602-610.

Hestbeck, J. B. 1995. Population study and management of Atlantic Flyway Canada geese. Journal of Applied Statistics 22:877-890.

Hestbeck, J. B., and R. A. Malecki 1989. Estimated survival rates of Canada Geese within the Atlantic Flyway. Journal of Wildlife Management 53:91-96.

Heusman, H W, and J. R. Sauer. 2000. The northeastern states' waterfowl breeding population survey. Wildlife Society Bulletin 28:355-364.

Hilborn, R., and C. J. Walters. 1992. Quantitative fisheries stock assessment: choice, dynamics and uncertainty. Chapman and Hall, New York, New York. 570pp.

Johnson, F. A. 2003. Population dynamics of ducks other than mallards in midcontinent North America. Draft. Fish and Wildlife Service, U.S. Dept. Interior, Washington, D.C. 15pp.

Johnson, F. A., J. A. Dubovsky, M. C. Runge, and D. R. Eggeman. 2002a. A revised protocol for the adaptive harvest management of eastern mallards. Fish and Wildlife Service, U.S. Dept. Interior, Washington, D.C. 13pp. [online] URL: http://migratorybirds.fws.gov/reports/ahm02/emal-ahm-2002.pdf.

Johnson, F. A., W. L. Kendall, and J. A. Dubovsky. 2002b. Conditions and limitations on learning in the adaptive management of mallard harvests. Wildlife Society Bulletin 30:176-185.

Johnson, F. A., C. T. Moore, W. L. Kendall, J. A. Dubovsky, D. F. Caithamer, J. R. Kelley, Jr., and B. K. Williams. 1997. Uncertainty and the management of mallard harvests. Journal of Wildlife Management 61:202-216.

Johnson, F. A., and B. K. Williams. 1999. Protocol and practice in the adaptive management of waterfowl harvests. Conservation Ecology 3(1): 8. [online] URL: http://www.consecol.org/vol3/iss1/art8.

Johnson, F. A., B. K. Williams, J. D. Nichols, J. E. Hines, W. L. Kendall, G. W. Smith, and D. F. Caithamer. 1993. Developing an adaptive management strategy for harvesting waterfowl in North America. Transactions of the North American Wildlife and Natural Resources Conference 58:565-583.

Johnson, F. A., B. K. Williams, and P. R. Schmidt. 1996. Adaptive decision-making in waterfowl harvest and habitat management. Proceedings of the International Waterfowl Symposium 7:26-33.

Lubow, B. C. 1995. SDP: Generalized software for solving stochastic dynamic optimization problems. Wildlife Society Bulletin 23:738-742.

Martin, E. M. and P. I. Padding. 1998. Preliminary estimates of waterfowl harvest and hunter activity in the United States during the 1997 hunting season. Unpublished Administrative Report, U.S. Fish and Wildlife Service, Laurel, MD. 34pp.

Martin, E. M. and P. I. Padding. 1999. Preliminary estimates of waterfowl harvest and hunter activity in the United States during the 1998 hunting season. Unpublished Administrative Report, U.S. Fish and Wildlife Service, Laurel, MD. 34pp.

Martin, E. M. and P. I. Padding. 2000. Preliminary estimates of waterfowl harvest and hunter activity in the United States during the 1999 hunting season. Unpublished Administrative Report, U.S. Fish and Wildlife Service, Laurel, MD. 34pp.

Martin, E. M. and P. I. Padding. 2001. Preliminary estimates of waterfowl harvest and hunter activity in the United States during the 2000 hunting season. Unpublished Administrative Report, U.S. Fish and Wildlife Service, Laurel, MD. 33pp.

Martin, E. M. and P. I. Padding. 2002. Preliminary estimates of waterfowl harvest and hunter activity in the United States during the 2001 hunting season. Unpublished Administrative Report, U.S. Fish and Wildlife Service, Laurel, MD. 33pp.

Meyer, R., and R. B. Millar. 1999. BUGS in Bayesian stock assessments. Canadian Journal of Fisheries and Aquatic Sciences 56: 1078-1087.

Millar, R. B., and R. Meyer. 2000. Non-linear state space modeling of fisheries biomass dynamics by using Metropolis-Hastings within Gibbs sampling. Applied Statistics 49: 327-342.

Munro, R. E., and C. F. Kimball. 1982. Population ecology of the mallard. VII. Distribution and derivation of the harvest. U.S. Fish and Wildlife Service Resource Publication 147. 127pp.

Nichols, J. D., F. A. Johnson, and B. K. Williams. 1995. Managing North American waterfowl in the face of uncertainty. Annual Review of Ecology and Systematics 26:177-199.

Puterman, M. L. 1994. Markov decision processes: discrete stochastic dynamic programming. John Wiley & Sons, Inc. New York, New York. 649pp.

Quinn T. J. II, and R. B. Deriso. 1999. Quantitative fish dynamics. Oxford University Press, New York, New York. 542pp.

Raveling, D. G. 1981. Survival, experience, and age in relation to breeding success of Canada geese. Journal of Wildlife Management 45:817-829.

Raveling, D. G., J. S. Sedinger, and D. S. Johnson. 2000. Reproductive success and survival in relation to experience during the first two years in Canada geese. Condor 102:941-945.

Runge, M. C., F. A. Johnson, J. A. Dubovsky, W. L. Kendall, J. Lawrence, and J. Gammonley. 2002. A revised protocol for the adaptive harvest management of midcontinent mallards. Fish and Wildlife Service, U.S. Dept. Interior, Washington, D.C. 28pp. [online] URL: http://migratorybirds.fws.gov/reports/ahm02/MCMrevise2002.pdf.

Spiegelhalter, D. J., A. Thomas, N. Best, and D. Lunn. 2003. WinBUGS 1.4 User manual. MRC Biostatistics Unit, Institute of Public Health, Cambridge, UK.

U.S. Fish and Wildlife Service. 2000a. Adaptive harvest management: 2000 duck hunting season. U.S. Dept. Interior, Washington. D.C. 43pp. [online] URL: http://migratorybirds.fws.gov/reports/ahm00/ahm2000.pdf.

U.S. Fish and Wildlife Service. 2000*b*. Framework-date extensions for duck hunting in the United States: projected impacts & coping with uncertainty, U.S. Dept. Interior, Washington, D.C. 8pp. [online] URL: http://migratorybirds.fws.gov/reports/ahm01/fwassess.pdf.

U.S. Fish and Wildlife Service. 2001. Adaptive harvest management: 2001 duck hunting season. U.S. Dept. Interior, Washington. D.C. 47pp. [online] URL: http://migratorybirds.fws.gov/reports/ahm01/ahm2001.pdf.

U.S. Fish and Wildlife Service. 2002. Adaptive harvest management: 2002 duck hunting season. U.S. Dept. Interior, Washington. D.C. 34pp. [online] URL: http://migratorybirds.fws.gov/reports/ahm02/2002-AHM-report.pdf.

U.S. Fish and Wildlife Service. 2003. Adaptive harvest management: 2003 duck hunting season. U.S. Dept. Interior, Washington. D.C. 30pp. [online] URL: http://migratorybirds.fws.gov/reports/ahm03/2003-AHM-report.pdf.

Walters, C. J. 1986. Adaptive management of renewable resources. MacMillan Publ. Co., New York, N.Y. 374pp.

Wilkins, K., and M. Otto 2003. Trends in duck breeding populations 1955-2003. Unpublished Administrative Report, U.S. Fish and Wildlife Service, Laurel, MD. 19pp.

Williams, B. K., and F. A. Johnson. 1995. Adaptive management and the regulation of waterfowl harvests. Wildlife Society Bulletin 23:430-436.

Williams, B. K., F. A. Johnson, and K. Wilkins. 1996. Uncertainty and the adaptive management of waterfowl harvests. Journal of Wildlife Management 60:223-232.

APPENDIX A: AHM Working Group

(Note: This list includes only permanent members of the AHM Working Group. Not listed here are numerous persons from federal and state agencies that assist the Working Group on an ad-hoc basis.)

Coordinator:

Fred Johnson
U.S. Fish & Wildlife Service
7920 NW 71st Street
Gainesville, FL 32653
phone: 352-264-3532
fax: 352-378-4956
e-mail: fred_a_johnson@fws.gov

USFWS representatives:

Bob Blohm (Region 9)
U.S. Fish and Wildlife Service
4401 N Fairfax Drive
MS MSP-4107
Arlington, VA 22203
phone: 703-358-1966
fax: 703-358-2272
e-mail: robert_blohm@fws.gov

Brad Bortner (Region 1)
U.S. Fish and Wildlife Service
911 NE 11th Ave.
Portland, OR 97232-4181
phone: 503-231-6164
fax: 503-231-2364
e-mail: brad_bortner@fws.gov

Frank Bowers (Region 4)
U.S. Fish and Wildlife Service
1875 Century Blvd., Suite 345
Atlanta, GA 30345
phone: 404-679-7188
fax: 404-679-7285
e-mail: frank_bowers@fws.gov

Dave Case (contractor)
D.J. Case & Associates
607 Lincolnway West
Mishawaka, IN 46544
phone: 574-258-0100
fax: 574-258-0189
e-mail: dave@djcase.com

John Cornely (Region 6)
U.S. Fish and Wildlife Service
P.O. Box 25486, DFC
Denver, CO 80225
phone: 303-236-8155 (ext 259)
fax: 303-236-8680
e-mail: john_cornely@fws.gov

Ken Gamble (Region 9)
U.S. Fish and Wildlife Service
101 Park DeVille Drive, Suite B
Columbia, MO 65203
phone: 573-234-1473
fax: 573-234-1475
e-mail: ken_gamble@fws.gov

George Haas (Region 5)
U.S. Fish and Wildlife Service
300 Westgate Center Drive
Hadley, MA 01035-9589
phone: 413-253-8576
fax: 413-253-8480
e-mail: george_haas@fws.gov

Jeff Haskins (Region 2)
U.S. Fish and Wildlife Service
P.O. Box 1306
Albuquerque, NM 87103
phone: 505-248-6827 (ext 30)
fax: 505-248-7885
e-mail: jeff_haskins@fws.gov

Bob Leedy (Region 7)
U.S. Fish and Wildlife Service
1011 East Tudor Road
Anchorage, AK 99503-6119
phone: 907-786-3446
fax: 907-786-3641
e-mail: robert_leedy@fws.gov

Jerry Serie (Region 9)
U.S. Fish and Wildlife Service
11510 American Holly Drive
Laurel, MD 20708
phone: 301-497-5851
fax: 301-497-5885
e-mail: jerry_serie@fws.gov

Dave Sharp (Region 9)
U.S. Fish and Wildlife Service
P.O. Box 25486, DFC
Denver, CO 80225-0486
phone: 303-275-2386
fax: 303-275-2384
e-mail: dave_sharp@fws.gov

Bob Trost (Region 9)
U.S. Fish and Wildlife Service
911 NE 11th Ave.
Portland, OR 97232-4181
phone: 503-231-6162
fax: 503-231-6228
e-mail: robert_trost@fws.gov

Steve Wilds (Region 3)
U.S. Fish and Wildlife Service
1 Federal Drive
Ft. Snelling, MN 55111-4056
phone: 612-713-5480
fax: 612-713-5393
e-mail: steve_wilds@fws.gov

Canadian Wildlife Service representatives:

Dale Caswell
Canadian Wildlife Service
123 Main St. Suite 150
Winnepeg, Manitoba, Canada R3C 4W2
phone: 204-983-5260
fax: 204-983-5248
e-mail: dale.caswell@ec.gc.ca

Eric Reed
Canadian Wildlife Service
351 St. Joseph Boulevard
Hull, QC K1A OH3, Canada
phone: 819-953-0294
fax: 819-953-6283
e-mail: eric.reed@ec.gc.ca

Flyway Council representatives:

Scott Baker (Mississippi Flyway)
Mississippi Dept. of Wildlife, Fisheries, and Parks
P.O. Box 378
Redwood, MS 39156
 phone: 601-661-0294
fax: 601-364-2209
e-mail: mahannah1@aol.com

Diane Eggeman (Atlantic Flyway)
Florida Fish and Wildlife Conservation Commission
8932 Apalachee Pkwy.
Tallahassee, FL 32311
phone: 850-488-5878
fax: 850-488-5884
e-mail: diane.eggeman@fwc.state.fl.us

Jim Gammonley (Central Flyway)
Colorado Division of Wildlife
317 West Prospect
Fort Collins, CO 80526
phone: 970-472-4379
fax: 970-472-4457
e-mail: jim.gammonley@state.co.us

Mike Johnson (Central Flyway)
North Dakota Game and Fish Department
100 North Bismarck Expressway
Bismarck, ND 58501-5095
phone: 701-328-6319
fax: 701-328-6352
e-mail: mjohnson@state.nd.us

Don Kraege (Pacific Flyway)
Washington Dept. of Fish and Wildlife
600 Capital Way North
Olympia. WA 98501-1091
phone: 360-902-2509
fax: 360-902-2162
e-mail: kraegdkk@dfw.wa.gov

Bruce Pollard (Atlantic Flyway)
Ontario Ministry of Natural Resources
P.O. Box 7000
300 Water Street
North Peterborough, ON K9J 8M5, Canada
phone: 705-755-1932
fax: 705-755-1900
e-mail: bruce.pollard@mnr.gov.on.ca

Dan Yparraguirre (Pacific Flyway)
California Dept. of Fish and Game
1812 Ninth Street
Sacramento, CA 95814
phone: 916-445-3685
e-mail: dyparraguirre@dfg.ca.gov

Guy Zenner (Mississippi Flyway)
Iowa Dept. of Natural Resources
1203 North Shore Drive
Clear Lake, IA   50428
phone: 515/357-3517, ext. 23
fax: 515-357-5523
e-mail: gzenner@netins.net

APPENDIX B: Modeling Midcontinent Mallard Harvest Rates

We modeled harvest rates of midcontinent mallards within a Bayesian statistical framework (USFWS 2003). We developed a set of models to predict harvest rates under each regulatory alternative as a function of the harvest rates observed under the liberal alternative, using historical information relating harvest rates to various regulatory alternatives. We modeled the probability of regulation-specific harvest rates (h) based on normal distributions with the following parameterizations:

Closed: $p(h_C) \sim N(\mu_C, v_C^2)$

Restrictive: $p(h_R) \sim N(\gamma_R \mu_L, v_R^2)$

Moderate: $p(h_M) \sim N(\gamma_M \mu_L + \delta_f, v_M^2)$

Liberal: $p(h_L) \sim N(\mu_L + \delta_f, v_L^2)$

For the restrictive and moderate alternatives we introduced the parameter γ to represent the relative difference between the harvest rate observed under the liberal alternative and the moderate or restrictive alternatives. Based on this parameterization, we are making use of the information that has been gained (under the liberal alternative) and are modeling harvest rates for the restrictive and moderate alternatives as a function of the mean harvest rate observed under the liberal alternative. We also considered the marginal effect of framework-date extensions under the moderate and liberal alternatives by including the parameter δ_f.

In order to update the probability distributions of harvest rates realized under each regulatory alternative, we first needed to specify a prior probability distribution for each of the model parameters. These distributions represent prior beliefs regarding the relationship between each regulatory alternative and the expected harvest rates. We used a normal distribution to represent the mean and a scaled inverse-chi-square distribution to represent the variance of the normal distribution of the likelihood. For the mean (μ) of each harvest-rate distribution associated with each regulatory alternative, we use the predicted mean harvest rates provided in USFWS (2000a:13-14), assuming uniformity of regulatory prescriptions across flyways. We set prior values of each standard deviation (v) equal to 20% of the mean (CV = 0.2) based on an analysis by Johnson et al. (1997). We then specified the following prior distributions and parameter values under each regulatory package:

Closed (in U.S. only):

$$p(\mu_C) \sim N(0.0088, \frac{0.0018^2}{6})$$

$$p(v_C^2) \sim Scaled\ Inv - \chi^2(6, 0.0018^2)$$

These closed-season parameter values are based on observed harvest rates in Canada during the 1988-93 seasons, which was a period of restrictive regulations in both Canada and the United States.

Restrictive:

$$p(\gamma_R) \sim N(0.51, \frac{0.15^2}{6})$$

$$p(v_R^2) \sim Scaled\ Inv - \chi^2(6, 0.0133^2)$$

Moderate:

$$p(\gamma_M) \sim N(0.85, \frac{0.26^2}{6})$$

$$p(v_M^2) \sim Scaled\ Inv - \chi^2(6, 0.0223^2)$$

For the harvest-rate distributions assumed under the restrictive and moderate regulatory packages, we specified that γ_R and γ_M are equal to the prior estimates of the predicted mean harvest rates under the restrictive and moderate alternatives divided by the prior estimates of the predicted mean harvest rates observed under the liberal alternative. Thus, these parameters act to scale the mean of the restrictive and moderate distributions in relation to the mean harvest rate observed under the liberal regulatory alternative. We further specified that the standard error of the normal distribution is based on a coefficient of variation for the mean equal to 0.3. The scale parameter of the inverse-chi- square distribution was set equal to the standard deviation of the harvest rate under the restrictive and moderate regulation alternatives, respectively.

Liberal:

$$p(\mu_L) \sim N(0.1305, \frac{0.0261^2}{6})$$

$$p(v_L^2) \sim Scaled\ Inv - \chi^2(6, 0.0261^2)$$

The prior distribution for the marginal effect of the framework-date extension was specified as:

$$p(\delta_f) \sim N(0.02, 0.01^2)$$

The prior distributions were multiplied by the likelihood functions based on the six years of data (under liberal regulations), and the resulting posterior distributions were evaluated with Markov Chain Monte Carlo simulation. Posterior estimates of model parameters and of annual harvest rates are provided in the following table:

Parameter	Estimate	SD	Parameter	Estimate	SD
μ_C	0.0088	0.0007	h_{1998}	0.1102	0.0113
v_C	0.0019	0.0005	h_{1999}	0.1002	0.0076
γ_R	0.5093	0.0616	h_{2000}	0.1264	0.0101
v_R	0.0129	0.0033	h_{2001}	0.1075	0.0113
γ_M	0.8509	0.1064	h_{2002}	0.1133	0.0060
v_M	0.0217	0.0055	h_{2003}	0.1134	0.0084
μ_L	0.1171	0.0077			
v_L	0.0225	0.0047			
δ_f	0.0129	0.0088